DEL RIO
QUEEN CITY OF THE RIO GRANDE

The first dam on San Felipe Creek is Madre Dam, shown here in the background under the railroad bridge. The Blue Hole pool behind the dam is a popular recreational spot. The creek runs through Moore Park.

THE
MAKING OF AMERICA
SERIES

DEL RIO

QUEEN CITY OF THE RIO GRANDE

DOUGLAS BRAUDAWAY

ARCADIA
PUBLISHING

Copyright © 2002 by Douglas Braudaway
ISBN 978-0-7385-2387-3

Published by Arcadia Publishing,
Charleston SC, Chicago IL, Portsmouth NH, San Francisco CA

Printed in the United States

Library of Congress control number: 2002106322

For all general information contact Arcadia Publishing at:
Telephone 843-853-2070
Fax 843-853-0044
E-Mail sales@arcadiapublishing.com
For customer service and orders:
Toll-Free 1-888-313-2665

Visit us on the Internet at www.arcadiapublishing.com

Front cover: *The Border Grocery occupied the northwest corner of Main and Garfield, where Del Rio National Bank now has its drive-through facilities. On the northeast corner is the Joseph Hyman Building whose upper floor was being used as a hotel. The smaller building directly north has been a bicycle shop and a furrier at different times. Here, the building is occupied by a hat shop that may also be a laundry. (Warren Studio.)*

CONTENTS

ACKNOWLEDGMENTS

With my previous two Arcadia books—both of which were photographic histories—this part of the book gave a list of the people and organizations that provided photographs. And I want to do that here. Most of the images come from two places: Warren Studio and my own postcard collection. I would like to thank Rosantina Calvetti and Nellie Fuentes for the great amount of work they did finding and reproducing so many old prints of Del Rio. Thanks also to Charles Carlson, the Kinney County Clerk's Office, Laughlin Air Force Base, Dudley Martin, Rob Poteat and the Laughlin Air Force Base History Office, the Sanborn Map Company, the Southwestern Oblate Historical Archives, Daisy and Guy Speer, the Texas General Land Office, Texas Tech's Southwest Collection, the Val Verde County Clerk's Office, Val Verde County Historical Commission, and the Whitehead Memorial Museum.

The documentary sources come from a variety of archives and collections. I am grateful to all the archivists who have helped me track down sources, but I would also like to thank the people who have placed materials in those archives. So many times questions about history cannot be answered authoritatively because source documentation has been lost. As any historian will tell you, you never have it all. Still, many people have written about Del Rio or about topics that include Del Rio, and a great many of them have been incorporated into this and noted in bibliographic essays at the end of the book.

I also want to thank my father, Jessie Braudaway. The computer on which this was typed came from him, as did a more recent laptop, which has made researching various archives much easier. I also thank my wife Willie for proofreading and suggesting many improvements. Without the two of them, much of this work could not have been done.

Many more photographs of Del Rio's history are found in *Val Verde County* and *Railroads of Western Texas: San Antonio to El Paso*, published by Arcadia in 1999 and 2000.

1. WATER ON THE ROAD

Del Rio's history covers a small period of time compared with this area's prehistoric habitation. Archeological evidence demonstrates that human beings have lived in the area now known as Val Verde County for thousands of years. Visitors to Del Rio see the apparently barren landscape and conclude that people could not have lived here on the edge of the Chihuahuan Desert. However, the earliest recorded observations described the area as covered with long expanses of waving grass replete with game animals in 1590; these same descriptions were made in the 1890s as well.

Val Verde County is covered with numerous natural springs and seeps—at least 43 recorded sites. Many of these springs are partial sources of streams and rivers, including the Devil's River. Goodenough Springs, now under Amistad Reservoir, are the third largest springs in Texas, and San Felipe Springs are fourth. San Felipe Springs and the rest are the westernmost of the Balcones Fault Zone springs, a line of springs including those at New Braunfels (Texas's largest), San Marcos (the second largest), and Austin. The San Felipe Springs, however, are more important to the local environment than those farther east because Del Rio's area rainfall is much less than the more eastern cities' rainfall.

The Springs are commonly said to gush 90 million gallons a minute, but that flow is rare—only occurring after months of good rain over the watershed. The normal flow is less. Even during drought years though, the Springs flow prodigiously: 37 million gallons a day in 1963 and 38 million gallons in 1996. The aquifer is the same Edwards Aquifer on which San Antonio relies, but a rock upthrust near Brackettville in Kinney County divides the water-bearing formation in two.

Water wells dug south of the Springs, or more properly, south of the "bad water line" usually flow full of minerals or sulfur. With no natural outlet for the aquifer south of San Felipe Springs, the groundwater dissolves and absorbs minerals, resulting in well water having a strange taste and smell. (A mineral well on the property of the Mason-Foster House on Hudson Street in the southern portion of town provided water for mineral baths during the early part of the 1900s.) Water north of the line (approximately Highway 90) runs clean and clear because the water does not stagnate underground.

The springs and surface waters—Devil's River, Pecos River, the Rio Grande, and many small rivers in Mexico—made the Val Verde County area a fertile environment.

Archeological evidence indicates that human beings were in Val Verde as early as 11,300 years ago. Manmade objects found with bones of extinct animals inform archaeologists that ancient man hunted native camels, mammoths, and giant bison.

Bonfire Shelter, west of Del Rio near Langtry, is one of the oldest major archeological sites in Val Verde County. The Bonfire site is special in at least a couple of aspects. While Bonfire Shelter is not the only bison kill site in North America, it is the southernmost site and the oldest site known. The remains at Bonfire Shelter demonstrate the incredible adaptability of humankind. At a cleft in Mile Canyon 10,500 years ago, hunters drove a herd of giant bison, properly called *Bison bison antiquus*, over the canyon rim. The bison fell to the floor, and afterward the hunters butchered the animal carcasses. On two other occasions, hunters repeated the feat at this site.

While Bonfire is unique to Val Verde, the county has hundreds of other known archeological sites. Those ancient peoples who first settled Val Verde (in a semi-permanent manner) established themselves by 8,500 to 8,000 years ago. The occupation of the area is considered to have been continuous from that time into historic times. Human habitation along Del Rio's San Felipe Creek for 3,300 years has been proven by archeological study; the research suggests evidence of older habitation may lie as yet undiscovered. However, little is known about historically

This Noah Rose photo highlights the water that led to the creation of Del Rio. San Felipe Creek has brought visitors to this area for millennia. (Whitehead Memorial Museum.)

The Creek flows from a group of springs by the same name—the San Felipe Springs. The main groups of springs are situated on a tract of land that is now the Del Rio Municipal Golf Course. (Whitehead Memorial Museum.)

identified tribal groups that may have lived in the Del Rio area.

The earliest historical documentation of Native Americans in Southwest Texas was made by the Spanish. During one of their expeditions, the names of many groups were listed. Among them were the Ororosos (Horrible Ones), the Gediodos (Stinking Ones), the Arcos (Bow Makers), and the Conchumuchas (People of Many Shells). These peoples were probably Jumano bands (who, by the 1700s, had joined with Apache groups), loose bands of Apaches and, perhaps, Coahuiltecan bands.

The Jumano peoples probably traveled through the Val Verde area, but were described by the Spanish as living in the river valleys along the Rio Grande west of Val Verde County. However, they were known to travel long distances to trade, visit, and hunt. Several divisions of Apaches are known to have operated in the area of Southwest Texas. Linguistically, Apaches are part of the Athapaskans of the American Northwest and Canada who migrated southward. The Mescalero, Lipan, and—to a lesser extent—the Kiowa Apache lived in Southwest Texas and probably in Val Verde; however, very little is known of them. Speculation suggests that Apache archeological sites have been found, but not recognized as such.

The first Spanish exploration of the Del Rio area occurred during 1590 when Gaspar Castaño de Sosa crossed the Rio Grande near Del Rio on his way to establish settlements in the New Mexico area. The earliest reported semi-permanent Spanish activity in the Del Rio area occurred between the years 1672

9

and 1675. For three years, Fray Juan Larios taught Catholicism on the Texas side of the Rio Grande in the areas of Kinney and Maverick Counties. The local legend that these Spanish priests celebrated mass and named San Felipe Springs in 1675 is, to date, undocumented and unproven. Other Spaniards followed, establishing trails or presidios, but few stayed in the area, and they usually left in short order. The terrain was too rugged and the support population too distant for Spanish settlements to be permanently established.

Governor Blas de la Garza Falcón explored the area during 1735 and 1736, having been instructed to find a site to establish a presidio near the Apache trails from Texas into the settlements of Coahuila and Nueva Vizcaya (Chihuahua) to check Apache raids. Garza Falcón chose a site on the San Diego River, south of the Rio Grande and near modern-day Ciudad Acuña. The site was quickly abandoned and relocated to a point near the present-day city of Melchior Múzquiz, where the soldiers could better protect the communities in that area. In 1767, during a reorganization of the presidios into a single unified line of defense, Falcón's presidio was moved back to the Rio Grande near its original location but with a new name: Aguaverde. However, by 1783, the northernmost presidios were once again considered too far from the settlements to be useful, and Aguaverde was removed southward to San Fernando de Austria (modern Zaragoza, Coahuila, about 25 miles from Piedras Negras).

This last move ended the Spanish presence in the Del Rio area. With the exception of the ill-fated Dolores Colony in neighboring Kinney County, no other exploration was recorded until after 1845, when Texas became a part of the United States and American interests focused on the newly acquired American Southwest.

The first recorded American entry into the area was made by John Coffee Hays. Jack Hays was a former Texas Ranger, a surveyor, and a popular San Antonio citizen. Hays led the Chihuahua–El Paso Expedition of 1848 with the objective of linking San Antonio to those two cities. Texans wanted to capture the trade between the northern states of Mexico and the United States (through Missouri and the New Mexico Territory). After great trials and tribulations and receiving aid and advice from some Mescalero Apaches on the way, the expedition arrived at Fort Leaton near the modern town of Presidio, and by December the group made it back to San Antonio. They had not traveled all the way to Chihuahua City or El Paso, but they established trails that connected Fort Leaton with both cities. Hays and his party had proven that a road from San Antonio (through Del Rio) to points west was possible.

The United States Army followed Hays, sending a number of expeditions west through Del Rio's part of the state. Two army lieutenants with the Bureau of Topographical Engineers, William F. Smith and H.C. Whiting, led their party out of San Antonio on February 12, 1849. They were to locate a suitable road to El Paso and find sites for military posts. With them traveled a group of emigrants on their way to California. On the outbound trip they traveled through the Texas Hill Country north of Val Verde, arriving in El Paso on April 12, 1849. Because the route lacked sufficient water, the party began its return on April 19 by a more southerly route—through Val Verde, which Smith later concluded was the better, "more practical" route. The U.S. Army then sent Major Jefferson Van Horn with six companies of the Third Infantry and a government train of 275 wagons and 2,500 hooved animals to test the route. Jack Hays accompanied this expedition. Hays and the rest camped at San Felipe Creek, and some of the men "considered this the most attractive stream on their trip," an opinion often written in journals and letters by travelers in subsequent years. The company traveled from San Antonio during the summer and early autumn arriving in El Paso on September 8, 1849. Nearing El Paso, the company found fresh fruits and vegetables for sale along the Rio Grande, mitigating the difficulty of the final leg of the trip. Van Horn proved "beyond any shadow of doubt" that the route that became the San Antonio–El Paso Road was reliable "as a major transportation link for the settlement of Texas and the western United States."

Another army reconnaissance through Val Verde was made by Captain S.G. French in the spring of 1849 following the same basic route. Some of the "Forty-Niners" used the newly established southern route to travel to the California gold fields. Merchants with wagon trains proceeded from the ports of Galveston, Indianola, and New Orleans on their way west—and back again. The first U.S. mail went through to El Paso in 1851. The rider was captured by Native Americans, who took his saddle and provisions, but left his life and letters intact. Later that year, Henry Skillman "decided to set things on a more secure and

Rough Canyon on the Devil's River was difficult to negotiate for explorers such as Hays, but it has now become a popular site for people wanting to live in the country. (Whitehead Memorial Museum.)

systematic basis." He won a mail contract from the U.S. government for Route No. 6401 from San Antonio to El Paso. Skillman also delivered people from Bexar to El Paso for $100 and to Santa Fe for $125. All of this was possible because of the water provided by San Felipe Springs, the Devil's River, and the other springs scattered across Val Verde County.

Another of the more famous Texas tracks is known as the Chihuahua Trail or the Chihuahua Road. At one end of the road was Indianola, the major eighteenth-century Texas seaport. The road overlapped the SA-EP Road to a point west of Del Rio where it turned southward to Presidio, Ojinaga, and Chihuahua City in Mexico. Hundreds of wagon trains followed the road west and south. Luxury goods and manufactured items were taken to northern Mexico. The wagons returned through Val Verde to the Gulf Coast carrying Mexican silver, copper, and lead. The roads remained active into the 1880s, when they were replaced by the railroad line that was built along much of the same route as these pioneer roads.

The spring-fed Devil's River flows with cool, clear water between high, rocky cliffs. The trail west—most commonly known as the San Antonio–El Paso Road—turned north to follow the water sources. Without this water, travelers may not have been able to traverse Southwest Texas. (Warren Studio.)

2. An Oasis in the Wilderness

Despite the high traffic flow by merchants and soldiers through the Del Rio area, permanent settlement did not happen before the American Civil War. By 1859, a man named Johnson had settled on San Felipe Creek and was living with his wife and two of his children. Zenas R. Bliss of the United States Army stationed at Fort Hudson on the Devil's River was surprised to find anyone living so far west. This early family must have packed up shortly after Bliss rode through because no home or family was mentioned in the soldier accounts of 1861.

As Confederate soldiers returned in 1862 from the New Mexico theater of war to San Antonio and points east, at least one of them recorded the presence of another pioneer family settled at San Felipe Springs. The family provided food and buttermilk for the soldiers and shelled corn for their mounts.

This was the family of James Taylor and his wife Paula Losoya Taylor, who came to San Felipe Creek in 1862 along with her sister Refugio Losoya de Rivera. (Incidentally, the proper spelling of the sisters' name is "Losolla," which once appeared on Del Rio street signs.) Taylor was a rancher from Uvalde. The Taylor family only lived along San Felipe Creek part-time, not moving permanently until the late 1860s or early 1870s. While common reports state that the Taylors learned about the Springs area from one of his cowboys, Juan Galdero, such is not entirely the case. The vaquero (or cowboys), by all accounts, had been scouting for missing cattle and Kickapoo Native Americans, and he is reported to have said that the Springs "would supply water to both man and beast indefinitely." But Taylor, like any resident rancher in the area, would already have known something about the Springs; after all, he was grazing his cattle in the area. He would not have allowed his stock to roam in this vicinity unless he had known sufficient water was available. Furthermore, he would have known from the merchants and drivers coming back along the roads from El Paso and Chihuahua City through Uvalde about the traveling conditions west along the road. It is likely that Taylor had not actually observed the Springs himself until the vaquero suggested to him that the Springs would be a good location for a farming community.

At the time the Taylors settled in Val Verde, a disorganized "community" is reported to have existed along San Felipe Creek about half a mile from the Rio Grande. The place was called "Las Sapas," the name for shelters which were nothing more than holes dug into the ground with brush and branches covering the openings.

One description of a riverside dwelling that may be a sapa similar to those said to be along the San Felipe Creek was this on the Rio Grande near Eagle Pass:

> The front, looking out towards the river, and on the intervening garden-ground, is latticed with reeds, and cunningly veiled by the earth and herbage of the bank, but is still pleasantly pervious to the cheering breeze and fresh light of this genial climate. The other three sides are cut square and even from the solid earth, which is here a favorable admixture of sand and clay, and requires no other walls or support. On these rests the roof. Willow and sycamore poles of sufficient size and strength from side to side; and closely laid on these supporters is a cross carpet of reeds, which is again covered with a thick layer of grass and earth. . . . A plaster of mud, slightly tempered with lime . . . gives whiteness and finish to these earth walls.

The place was also called "El Salto." What the residents did while there has also been left unrecorded. *La Hacienda*, Del Rio's bicentennial scrapbook, records the following:

> This community never experienced any growth because its inhabitants were merely using it as a stepping stone. New residents kept moving in but at the same time others were moving out, working their way into other well established communities.

However, no names of "established communities" are specifically mentioned. The shelters of Las Sapas faded into history as their nomadic residents moved near the Losoya Hacienda, and these shelters were gone by the end of 1870.

The Las Sapas could not have been established for long prior to the arrival of the Taylors. Rio Grande explorer Harry Love reported plainly that "no settlements, either American or Mexican" existed upriver from Fort Duncan (Eagle Pass). None of the known journals written during the Civil War troop movements of 1861 and 1862 mention the existence of any Mexican community on the creek.

One reason a group of Mexicans would be living in the United States without attracting attention to themselves can be found in the Mexican social system. Debt slavery or "peon servitude" was common in Mexico. While not technically slavery, "it resembled slavery in its severity and virtual permanence." An American in Eagle Pass in the early 1850s speculated that the majority of the town's Mexican population were escapees from the system. Because Texas was part of the United States and the 1848 Treaty of Guadalupe Hidalgo allowed all Mexicans in the newly acquired United States territory to claim American citizenship, the American side of the Rio Grande offered freedom. Nevertheless, kidnapping of runaway peons by

The Taylor-Rivers House is recorded as the oldest home in Del Rio. The house stands on the corner of Hudson (once called Taylor Street) and Nicholson Streets.

Mexican bounty hunters was known to occur; "former peons on the American side probably felt insecure." Even American citizens of Mexican ancestry were subject to kidnapping. Hence, any former Mexican nationals might reasonably want to live away from Piedras Negras and other populated parts of the border.

The home of the Taylor family quickly became a community center, and the Taylors should be considered the founders of Del Rio. They built a house and began cultivating the soil. They grew many crops including sugar cane, which might not be the most obvious crop to modern, urban dwellers, but the American sweet tooth had already developed. The family built a sugar cane mill to process the cane. With a sugar supply, Paula Taylor made Mexican candy such as *piloncillos*. They also built a flour mill (needed for bread) and a gin (to separate cotton seeds from cotton fiber to make thread).

The Losoya Taylor Hacienda was the center of the economic community and the center of the religious community. The sisters arranged for Catholic Oblate Fathers from Eagle Pass to make monthly visits to the Losoya Hacienda at San Felipe Del Rio. The "residents of San Felipe . . . would cross the creek" to the Losoyas' "where the whole town would gather" for services. On later occasions, Catholic services were held in the home of Genevieve Wallen and a building formerly on the site of Brinkley Lumber Company's office grounds.

Services in private homes remained the practice until the 1890s, when Sacred Heart Parish was established. On November 15, 1891, the cornerstone of the church building was laid and blessed by Reverend J.M. Malmartel, and on August 19, 1892, the completed structure was blessed by Bishop Neraz. Reverend F.X. Brule O.M.I. was appointed the parish's first pastor in 1905.

This postcard, dating to the turn of the century, shows the Sacred Heart Church building before it was substantially remodeled and enlarged. The Rectory has been demolished and the Academy has been modernized. The "Iylesia de Messira" appears to be the building for the newly formed Our Lady of Guadalupe Parish.

After years of growth, the parish divided, and the eventual division into three parishes reflected the division of the town into three general neighborhoods: Sacred Heart Parish covered downtown Del Rio, Our Lady of Guadalupe Parish (1906) covered San Felipe, and St. Joseph's Parish (1927) was centered in the Chihuahua area of town.

The community did not become a real town until the natural resources of the area could be effectively harnessed. That began June 12, 1868, when James Taylor and some associates purchased 1,476 acres of land to form the San Felipe Agricultural, Manufacturing and Irrigation Company (SFAMI), which subsequently added about 2,640 acres of irrigatable land. The company purchased the land from the heirs of James Mitchell, a Texas Revolution soldier who had died in the Battle of San Jacinto. Texas, as the Republic and the State, often granted land bounties to soldiers in exchange for their service. Neither Mitchell nor his heirs are known to have lived on the land.

Eleven other sections of contiguous land were bought from the State of Texas. The springs that comprise San Felipe Springs are found in Survey No. 184, which was patented in the name of Sostenes Corrosco. From the Springs, San Felipe Creek flows in a southerly direction towards its confluence with the Rio Grande through Survey No. 153, patented in the name of Erastus Smith (known generally as "Deaf" Smith and remembered as the man who prevented the escape of the Mexican army at the Battle of San Jacinto).

The original purchasers of the James Mitchell grant were James Taylor, William C. Adams, Randolph Pafford, Don Jackson, Joseph Ney, and John P. Grove. By 1870, the SFAMI Company began construction of the first irrigation canal. Within a year, the Madre Ditch was completed, and several lateral ditches were completed the second year. In the first year of organization, interests in the project were sold by some of the shareholders. The men drew lots in order to choose their homesites, each consisting of 11 acres. Because of the shortage of lumber (which was brought by wagon from the Gulf Coast), most built their homes of adobe. Grove sold out to A.O. Strickland, and Jackson sold a half-interest to Joseph Ney. Strickland and Ney are recorded on the early company documents while their predecessors are not. Strickland, however, was killed by Native Americans in 1871, and Jackson, a captain in the United States Army, died in 1876.

The year 1875 was a good one for the company. By the end of that year, over 3,000 acres were under irrigated cultivation. The Old San Felipe Ditch, just over 2 miles in length, starts at Tardy Dam near Academy Street and stays near the Creek until veering through neighborhoods south of town.

The principal canal is the Madre Canal, which begins at the dam at Moore Park. Two and a third miles long, it meanders to a point at Mill and Canal Streets, follows Canal Street, disappears under Pecan and Main Street to reappear near Griner, swings under Garfield/Las Vacas, and continues towards the southwest.

Several other canals branch from the Madre Canal. The San Felipe Canal starts at Mill and Canal and meanders between Pecan and Main Streets through old Del Rio. It then follows Hudson Drive, in front of the Taylor-Rivers House, and then southwestward in front of the Brinkley Mansion. The St. Mary's Canal leaves the

Tardy Dam, also known as San Felipe Dam, is now the site of San Felipe Lions Club Park. The waterway in the foreground is the canal for which the dam was built. This second dam on San Felipe Creek channels water into the Old San Felipe Ditch to south Del Rio.

Madre at Griner Street to Nicholson and off towards the southwest. Both the San Felipe and St. Mary's are almost 2.5 miles long. The 2.75-mile Concepcion Canal branches from the Madre near Garfield School and veers westward out of town for 1.75 miles. The Swag K Canal leaves Madre near the intersection of Cannon and Warner Streets, travels west then south, and joins the Concepcion. It is less than a mile long.

The last canal is not associated with the others. The G. Bedell Moore Ditch leaves the Creek near Diaz Street, where it follows the curve of the creek to the southeast and then south for a distance of just over 3 miles. The dam itself was constructed in 1904 by one of Del Rio's most prolific builders, John Taini, and the canal itself appears on maps dated 1905.

The company's project was well-enough off that the owners applied to the state for a state-recognized charter under a new state law. The charter was approved by the secretary of state's office on October 13, 1875, for a 99-year period. The charter was renewed in 1975 for an indefinite period of time.

The Del Rio area provided a good climate for many different crops. Del Rioans grew the sugar cane already mentioned, alfalfa hay (for livestock), peaches and pears, pecans and figs, onions and corn, and other assorted vegetables. Because the community members grew most of their own food, houses in San Felipe were widely spaced with several acres of land between them.

A modern community cannot become a viable town without a number of sources for manufactured and retail goods. One of the most prominent early businessmen in Val Verde was John Perry, a man with an interesting history. John Perry came to San Felipe Del Rio in 1870 from Harris County, Texas. Earlier, in

The great pecan trees provided shade and cool temperatures. A gravel road graded from town to the Devil's River allowed Del Rioans to visit by automobile. (Whitehead Memorial Museum.)

The Perry Store is the oldest commercial structure in Del Rio and is now part of the Whitehead Memorial Museum. It is said that Perry's Store was the largest between San Antonio and El Paso. This photo appears to have been shot during the 1960s when the structure was converted into the city's museum. (Warren Studio.)

San Antonio, he was captured by General Woll in one of the 1842 raids and taken to the prison at Perote Castle, Mexico. After his release he married and made some money in business. He came to Val Verde for his health; he had tuberculosis, and a common treatment of the day was to move west to drier climates. He became a rancher and a businessman, opening his store in the early 1870s. With the growing community and the military post as customers, Perry was successful. His store is reported to have been the largest between San Antonio and El Paso in its day. After Perry died, his family held onto the property and refused to sell because of the property's historical value. It was finally sold on the condition that it be preserved as a historic site, at which time, the store building became the foundation of the Whitehead Memorial Museum, dedicated on October 9, 1962.

Other early store-owners included C.D. Broadbent, Henry Roach, Louis Lindheim, H.M. Block, and James McLymont. These men were not only merchants. For instance, McLymont was a successful rancher, "known from the Rio Grande to the Conchos, from the Colorado to the Davis Mountains." This ranching background gave him a particular advantage because he knew and understood the kinds of goods that were needed by a county full of ranchers.

One of the more famous local enterprises was the "Ice Plant," built about 1883 on San Felipe Creek just upstream from the point where Academy Street crosses it, between Pecan Street and the Creek. Originally, it manufactured ice in 50-pound blocks, a valuable commodity in Southwest Texas. Ice could preserve food, though it was first used to cool beer. The ice plant was also a gristmill, grinding grain from local farmers and from Mexico. Later, it became a power-generating plant. Coal, for fuel, was brought in from Eagle Pass by the railroad to Del Rio

Del Rio Light Plant and Steam Laundry, Del Rio, Tex.

The Del Rio Light Plant provided electrical power to the growing town. One of the buildings on the right is the first Del Rio Steam Laundry, opened by C.A. Chastang (before it burned and was relocated to Pecan and Broadway), who also served as Del Rio's mayor during 1921–1922.

and then by wagon to the plant to generate electricity. Sometimes during movies, the lights and projector in the old movie theater would go out leaving the public in the dark. During such blackouts, the public knew that the plant had run out of coal. Electricity was first used for lights only. Electrical production was so slight that plugging in an electric iron would brownout the town; therefore, electric irons were not allowed for many years. In later times the irons were allowed to be used between four and six in the afternoon.

During the antebellum years, American travelers often recorded attacks by Native Americans in the Val Verde area. Few friendly encounters like that between the Hays Expedition and the Mescalero Apaches, who directed them to safety, were recorded. In the early days of San Felipe Del Rio, fears of Native American attacks were common. However, the attacks seem to have been fewer than feared.

While no Native American is actually confirmed to have attacked San Felipe Del Rio, attacks and fights were fairly common in the canyons and hills of the surrounding countryside. One fight took place in the spring of 1873 between some cowboys rounding up strays between the Sycamore and Devil's and some unidentified Comanche. "Six cowpunchers and seven Comanches" constituted the total combatants; nevertheless, the fighting was fierce. The results were four dead Comanches, one dead cowpuncher, and one cowpuncher who was nearly scalped while yet alive. He survived, but with a "genuine" scar. Native Americans also attacked wagon trains hauling freight at many points along the San Antonio–El Paso and Chihuahua Roads. A wagon train under August Santleben was raided near Beaver Lake in 1870. The raiders roped the "bell mare," leading her away with Santleben's herd of horses behind. (The horses had been trained to follow a lead horse to simplify the drover's control over the herd.)

The last Native American attack in the county is said to have taken place in 1881, but a variety of sources repeatedly give that year without any particular citation. In most sources, details are non-existent, but it seems that in that year near Comstock, the bodies of ten victims of an attack were found at the ominous-sounding Dead Man's Pass, an appellation that still appears on modern topographical maps. News was sent to Fort Clark, and soldiers arrived to bury the dead. Nevertheless, fights with Native Americans occurred at least as late as 1883:

> News has just reached our town of a fight between three Indians and one Mexican herder. The fight occurred at ten o'clock this morning (January 23), six miles northeast of Del Rio and resulted in the death of one Indian. The body was seen by the following citizens, H.J. Russel, J.H. Windset and Fritz Schrier, who are just in from the scene, and they say it is true without a doubt, and the dead body is that of an Indian.

A follow-up story stated that the dead individual was "no ordinary personage" but a "warrior of note."

While reports of Native American attacks were sparse, fear of them seems to have had real effects on the town. In the early years the town founders built a stockade on Main Street to guard against attacks from Native Americans and Mexicans. In early Del Rio, "Narrow streets were considered safer from Indian attacks." One other point oft repeated was that like many frontier towns, Del Rio had its share of saloons, and then some: "There were saloons in almost every block."

Nevertheless, early reports of life in Del Rio included many pleasant remarks. The mouth of the Devil's River was only twelve short miles away, and people would take buggy trips to picnic or camp out under the "magnificent" pecan trees. On hot days, swimming holes along the river and San Felipe Creek were available for a dip, and bicycles were popular. Wild game including turkeys were still common. Fish were plentiful in the rivers, and tales of treasure prompted expeditions to Sugar Loaf Mountain south of town.

There are many stories about this most familiar of Val Verde landmarks: Round Mountain. This steep-sided, cone-shaped hill south of Del Rio has gone by many names: Sugar Loaf Mound and Sugar Loaf Mountain, La Loma de la Cruz, or simply La Loma. Paula Losoya Taylor was the owner of the hill and the surrounding land, and she is the person who placed the original cross on the hill.

She put the cross there because, according to one legend, a number of people were killed at the hill. Townspeople fought a group of Mexican rebels coming north to steal horses. Some number of rebel bandits were killed in the fight and later buried at the foot of the hill. "Doña Paula had a cross erected and placed on the top of the hill to recognize the fact that it was hallowed ground since people were buried there." From that time the site has been known as La Loma de la Cruz or, in English, the Hill of the Cross.

One of the wildest tales is that La Loma holds "the treasure of Montezuma," one of the last rulers of the Aztec Empire. With the approach of Cortes and his Spanish conquistadors, vast riches were taken out of the capital city and hidden. Many places from Mexico City north lay claim to this treasure. According to one version of the local story, "once a year the mountain will open up for a short time" showing its hidden wealth. "Anyone there can run inside and take out what he can carry. If one gets greedy or takes too long to gather the treasure, the mountain will close up and trap him until the next year or until he dies!" Perhaps slow movers are the source of some of the ghosts that are supposed to haunt the hill. The cross on the hill has been said to have been placed there to placate these ghostly presences.

Another tale says that in years past Mexican bandits raided and robbed ranches in Mexico. They hauled away as much gold and silver as they were able to carry, enough that they needed a place to hide the loot so they could travel more quickly. They crossed the Rio Grande at a point familiar to one of the bandits—where San Felipe Creek flowed into the Rio Grande. Round Mountain, they surmised, made a good, recognizable landmark—"the perfect spot to make a 'round mountain' or 'mound' out of their treasures." The bandits piled their ill-gotten gains together and covered the pile with soil and rock dug out of the banks of the creek, and returned to Mexico. The story does not explain why the bandits never returned to reclaim their treasure.

The American Constitution requires the government to count all of the people in the United States every ten years for purposes of Congressional representation.

Sugar Loaf Mountain is more commonly known as Round Mountain or La Loma de la Cruz. The artificial-looking shape with steep slopes has spawned many stories of buried treasure and supernatural activity. (Whitehead Memorial Museum.)

The first Census to include the Del Rio area occurred in 1870. San Felipe Del Rio was counted in Kinney County in the middle of August.

Mexican-born persons made up the majority of the people and families in the community. The landowners were predominantly American-born; land ownership is indicated by the occupation "Farmer" as opposed to "Farm laborer." Only four people were noted as "Black"—all of them old enough that they might have been born into slavery. The three females were all listed as "Domestic servant," and the male as a "Laborer" (as distinct from "Farm Laborer").

Some 34 households were found in San Felipe Del Rio. All six American-born heads-of-households were listed as "Farmers." Nearly all, 24 of 28, of the Spanish-surnamed heads-of-household were listed as "Farm Laborer." One was an "Overseer [of] hands," two others were "Sheep Herdsman," and one was a land-owning "Farmer." The wife (and mother) of each household was listed as "Keeping house." A few households were occupied by two families or a family with live-in singles. Fourteen households included adults with different surnames in the household. Three households were occupied by adult men only, all "Farm Laborers" or "Sheep Herdsmen." In the town one person each was listed as "Clerk in Store," "Teacher," "Herdsman," "Blacksmith," "Carpenter," "Artist," "Overseer [of] hands," and "Cattle hunter." Four men were listed as "Sheep Herdsman," and one as "Sheepherder."

The population count for the community was 146. The adults (aged 21 and up) numbered 90, but 1 underaged head-of-household and 3 wives make a total of 94. That leaves 52 minors.

The census list follows. Each household is grouped separately. The first column lists the names of the early Del Rioans, second is age, third is occupation, fourth is place of birth. The right-hand column notes the four who were "Black." Everyone else on the roster was noted as "White." The right-hand column also notes possible correct spellings for some of the written Spanish surnames.

Taylor, James H.	43	Farmer	Pennsylvania	
Paulina	38	Keeping house	Texas	
Felis	19	Clerk in store	Texas	
Losolla, Francis	17	At home	Texas	
Uroan, Julia	16	Domestic servant	Texas	(Black)
Villareal, Jose	22	Laborer	Mexico	
Losolla, Alphonso	24	Farmer	Texas	
Barbuita	20	At home	Mexico	
Hudson, William B.	49	Farmer	Georgia	
Juanita	30	Keeping house	Texas	
Martha	11		Texas	
Annie	9		Mexico	
Elisabeth	7		Mexico	
William	5		Mexico	

Hendrick	3		Texas	
Mary Ann	6 1/2		Texas	
Fuentes, Martina	48	At home	Texas	
Marting, Aloina	60	Teacher	Texas	
Aradondo, Antonio	38	Farm laborer	Mexico	[Arredondo?]
Filofila	28	Keeping house	Mexico	
Trinidad	7		Mexico	
Juanita	5		Mexico	
Solita	3		Mexico	
Santita	4 1/2		Texas	
Rosa, Tanislado	24	Farm laborer	Mexico	
Hubanks, Gabriel	24	Herdsman	Virginia	
Aradondo, Pablo	28	Farm laborer	Mexico	[Arredondo?]
Jesusa	30	Keeping house	Mexico	
Juanita	8		Mexico	
Dias, Juan	35	Farm laborer	Mexico	[Diaz?]
Petra	30	Keeping house	Mexico	
Eusibia	6		Mexico	
Lazero	4		Mexico	
Rodriguez, Juan	30	Farm laborer	Mexico	
Juana	30	Keeping house	Mexico	
Soria, Juan	28	Farm laborer	Mexico	
Encarnacion	28	Keeping house	Mexico	
Teodoro	1		Texas	
Marjildo	4 1/2		Texas	
Treviño, Francisco	32	Farm laborer	Mexico	
Santas	35	Keeping house	Mexico	
Hilario	19	Farm laborer	Mexico	
Butierez, Telesfono	40	Farm laborer	Mexico	[Gutierrez?]
Simon, Louis	23	Blacksmith	Texas	
Lonira	22	Keeping house	Texas	
Adams, William	45	Farmer	Tennessee	
Mary	38		Texas	
Sallie	8		Texas	
Maggie	6		Texas	
William	2		Texas	

McDonald, Lufnic	8		Texas	
Holliday, George C.	24	Farmer	Mexico	
Mary Jane	17	Keeping house	Texas	
Austin, Charles	28	Carpenter	Illinois	
Garza, Manuel	50	Farmer	Mexico	
Filipa	40	Keeping house	Mexico	
Pafford, Randolph	61	Farmer	North Carolina	
Mary	54	Keeping house	Tennessee	
John	27	Farmer	Tennessee	
Cynthia	23	At home	Tennessee	
Marian	21	Law student	Tennessee	
Jane	17	Domestic servant	Tennessee	(Black)
Luz	16	Domestic servant	Tennessee	(Black)
Philips, Samuel	37	Artist	Tennessee	
Hutchens, Wiley	35	Farm laborer	Georgia	
Roach, Alfred	30	Laborer	Tennessee	(Black)
Solice, Eusibio	35	Farm laborer	Mexico	
Dolores	36	Keeping house	Mexico	
Ramon, Candelario	26	Farm laborer	Mexico	

Del Rio's population continued to grow in the early years of the twentieth century. Many early written sources present the town as having a good economy and good standard of living. (Whitehead Memorial Museum.)

The Devil's River may have been horrible on the early explorers, but the area later became a popular site for picnics, swimming, fishing, and other recreational activities. Del Rioans rode the train and got off at Devil's River Station. (Whitehead Memorial Museum.)

Mariana	22	Keeping house	Mexico	
Bernaldina	4		Mexico	
Hernandez, A___	20	Farm laborer	Mexico	
Ramon	17	Farm laborer	Mexico	
Hernandez, Santiago	25	Farm laborer	Mexico	
Saba	22	Keeping house	Mexico	
Hilario	3		Mexico	
Mateo	10 1/2		Texas	
Valdez, Fabian	45	Farm laborer	Mexico	
Francisca	40	Keeping house	Mexico	
Aguerro, Francisco	35	Farm laborer	Mexico	[Aguero?]
Maria	22	Keeping house	Mexico	
Maxima	8		Mexico	
Nacaria	7		Mexico	
Jose	1		Texas	
Juarra, Pallonio	20	Laborer	Mexico	[Juarez?]
Vicinta	44	Keeping house	Mexico	
Sierra, Augustine	40	Overseer hands	Mexico	

Anacleta	38	Keeping house	Mexico	
Patrita	9		Mexico	
Vicenta	8		Mexico	
Juanita	3		Mexico	
Jose	20	Farm laborer	Mexico	
Galindo, Antonio	39	Sheep herdsman	Mexico	
Padea, Leandro	26	Farm laborer	Mexico	[Padilla?]
Camelita	28	Keeping house	Mexico	
Casimira	3		Texas	
Tobar, Guadalupe	22	Farm laborer	Mexico	[Tovar?]
Narcissa	33	Keeping house	Mexico	
Frutalco	3		Mexico	
Luna, Bernardino	26	Farm laborer	Mexico	
Josefa	20	Keeping house	Mexico	
Pastia, Pedro	35	Farm laborer	Mexico	
Margarito	23	Farm laborer	Mexico	
Rodriguez, Eufimio	49	Farm laborer	Mexico	
Valdores	47	Keeping house	Mexico	
Pasqual	8		Mexico	
Galindo, Juan	18	Farm laborer	Mexico	
Gonzales, Jose	22	Farm laborer	Mexico	
Perez, Manuel	48	Farm laborer	Mexico	
Bia, Juan	64	Farm laborer	Mexico	
Reyas	49	Keeping house	Mexico	
Salcido, Daria	22	At home	Mexico	
Andrada, Natriado	48	Farm laborer	Mexico	[Andrade?]
Juana	35	Keeping house	Mexico	
Rosalio	12		Mexico	
Roman	9		Mexico	
Delfina	5		Mexico	
Josefina	3		Mexico	
Miranda, Francisco	40	Farm laborer	Mexico	
Roberta	25	Keeping house	Mexico	
Mariana	5		Mexico	
Martina	4		Mexico	
Josefita	3		Mexico	
Rodrigo, Gregoria	50	At home	Mexico	

Maños, Juan	40	Sheep herdsman	Mexico	[Muñoz?]
Narcissa	35	Keeping house	Mexico	
Rafaela	7		Mexico	
Sibero	8	Sheep herdsman	Mexico	
Benita	5		Texas	
Eufermio	3		Texas	
Serapia	1		Texas	
Padea, Cricento	49	Sheep herdsman	Mexico	[Padilla?]
Valdez, Ramon	60	Sheep herdsman	Mexico	
Strickland, A.O.	48	Farmer	Pennsylvania	
Paulina	35	Keeping house	Tennessee	
Freeman	16		Texas	
John	16		Texas	
Gay	2		Texas	
Allen, Meslissa	14		Texas	
Frank	11		Texas	
Lettie	9		Texas	
Anderson, J.H.	88	Farmer	South Carolina	
Drager, William	20	Cattle hunter	Prussia	
Maldonado, Marcus	53	Farm laborer	Mexico	
Tomasa	52	Keeping house	Mexico	
Bernadino	18	Farm laborer	Mexico	
Josefa	4		Texas	
Escobedo, Barcilus	26	Farm laborer	Mexico	
Reyes	25	Keeping house	Mexico	
Torres, Dolores	10		Texas	
Maria	8		Texas	
Escobedo, Hijos	4		Texas	
Margarito	3		Texas	
Leon	3 1/2		Texas	
Luna, Antonio	70	Farm laborer	Mexico	
Boluscus, Abram	30	Farm laborer	Mexico	
Indolacio	26	Farm laborer	Mexico	
Pollonio	24	Farm laborer	Mexico	
Etarra, Miguel	31	Farm laborer	Mexico	[Yturria?]
Ramires, Antonio	46	Farm laborer	Mexico	[Ramirez?]
Martiana	40	Keeping house	Mexico	
Antonio	16	Farm laborer	Mexico	

Josefa	15	Mexico
Juan	11	Mexico
Iginio	7	Mexico
Imedio	2	Mexico

The following families lived in the vicinity of the San Felipe Del Rio community, but the census records do not state that they lived in the community. These families are not included in the data summary, but they may also have descendants in the area:

Ignacio Berrera and family
Juan Berrera and family
Simon Marjicas and family
Francisca Arras
Santiago Menchaca and family with Salvador Gomez
Pedro Aguila and family
Donaciano Almargia and family

The old iron bridge over San Felipe Creek connecting Canal Street with the Brown Plaza area had a wooden deck that thundered as horse's hooves struck the surface. The structure was replaced in the early 1930s.

3. THE ITALIAN COLONY

During the 1880s, a number of Italian families left Milan and came to the New World—also known as Del Rio. Their journey to Del Rio may have been precipitated by other Italians at nearby Fort Clark providing much of the masonry work (for barracks and officers' quarters) done during the 1870s. Though names are not recorded, Italian stonemasons are repeatedly reported as being "building contractors" and stoneworkers.

Post records indicate that some 31 carpenters, 49 stonemasons, and 23 quarrymen were on the payroll, though the number of Italians among them is unknown. "Some stayed in Brackett and some went to Del Rio . . . and made up the Italian colony of Del Rio." The stonemasons knew about Del Rio since they traveled through town frequently because of the poor quality of the stone from the Fort Clark quarry. Stone was hauled from a quarry located on the Devil's River on a road that passed through the town. The quarrymen would have stopped at the plentiful San Felipe Springs and noted the good soil along San Felipe Creek.

Meanwhile, during the late 1870s, a number of northern Italian families immigrated to Mexico encouraged by the immigration policies of President Porfirio Diaz. That Italian colony, however, quickly collapsed as a result of the Mexican government's failure to implement land allocation promises. Many Italian families relocated to Texas, though the Ferinos and the Ferrares stayed in Cuatro Cienegas in northern Mexico and there established a winery. American census records for Del Rio indicate an occasional Italian-Mexican marriage; sometimes an eldest child is recorded as having been born in Mexico with the younger ones born as native Texans.

The Italian colony included the Molinias in 1879, with the Seraphini families arriving in 1881 and 1884, Bolners in 1882, and Gerolas and Valientes in 1889. Other families arrived later: Tagliabue, Valenti, Marini, and Garoni. Little is known about Paul Comolli, an Italian who had already settled in town and was greeting the new arrivals. He did own a great deal of land along Las Vacas, and a railroad crossing, a cemetery, and a neighborhood were named for him.

Living in the San Antonio area, Frank Qualia learned about opportunities in San Felipe Del Rio. Most of the good land around San Antonio had already been settled, but the railroad was opening up land to the west. Qualia found the good, inexpensive land he sought in Val Verde. It was fertile and had a reliable supply of water.

Qualia arrived in Val Verde in 1881. He leased from the Losoya family while saving money to buy some land outright. Having bought his first 10 acres of land, Qualia farmed and harvested marketable crops such as cabbage, carrots, and leafy vegetables. But more importantly, he planted grapevines. His first vines were Lenoir, Black Spanish grapes. Vines of this type, seemingly well suited to the alkaline soil, were already growing when Qualia arrived. Lenoir grapes can be eaten off the vine and turned into jam or jelly, but they also can be made into red wine.

Texas law of the day required a vintner's license before a person could legally produce alcohol. Qualia acquired this license in 1883 and began his operation. He used adobe construction for his residence and business. Abode was cheap, and it moderated the temperature for the fermentation process. He imported a hand-operated winepress from Europe. Over the years, Qualia's Val Verde Winery produced, sold, and profited.

Prohibition proved to be a great setback to the Texas wine industry. In 1919, alcoholic beverages were made generally illegal in Texas. Prohibition put most Texas vineyards out of business, but Qualia held on by producing non-alcoholic goods and maintaining the vines. One exemption in Prohibition allowed alcohol to be used for sacramental purposes. Providing wine for Catholic religious services was one of Qualia's goals for the winery. Eventually, Prohibition was repealed,

Flooding is common along the Rio Grande and, despite damage to property and occasional loss of life, the flooding is partly responsible for the rich soil along Val Verde County's river bottoms. (Southwestern Oblate Historical Archives.)

but no other Texas vineyards were still in business. Consequently, the Val Verde Winery is the oldest continuously operated Texas vineyard and winery.

After Prohibition the second generation of Qualias relicensed the Val Verde Winery. Louis Qualia introduced a new, disease-resistant grape called the Herbemont. He also bought some Toulouse geese which, except during harvest, were allowed to wander the vineyard to eat weeds. (If left in the vineyards at harvest, the geese will eat the grapes.) With these and other improvements, grape production grew. After Prohibition some vineyards reopened, but all but one had once again closed down during the 1950s. The Val Verde Winery once again was the sole survivor. Louis Qualia's contributions to the industry earned him a plaque of appreciation awarded by the Texas Grape Growers Association. Louis Qualia died in 1981, but the plaque was presented to his son Thomas a year later.

Most of the Italians settling in Del Rio were farmers. John Taini farmed some land in Del Rio, but he is much better known as a stonemason. Taini was born to Gerolamo Taini and Lucia Prandelli in Rezzato, Brescia, Italy (near Milan), on November 1, 1854, and emigrated from Milan to the United States in 1880. Taini and G.B. Cassinelli, a friend and business partner, were recruited in their native country by an American building contractor to do stone construction in New York. Shortly after their arrival the project failed, and the two men went to work on the railroads. Later, they were hired by the federal government to construct several stone buildings at Fort Clark in Brackettville. When that work was completed, they moved to Del Rio, working on several projects including the Val Verde County Courthouse, which was constructed in 1887–1888.

Other Italian families grew their own grapes and made their own wine, but the Qualias were the only Del Rio viniculturists to make wine commercially. (Whitehead Memorial Museum.)

The Qualia Farm is one of many small farms and vineyards the Italians (among others) started in Del Rio. The bottomland between San Felipe Creek and the Rio Grande has grown nearly everything from wheat to corn, from citrus to sugar cane, and grapes. This 1906 photo shows intercropping—the practice of growing two different crops on the same tract of land. (Whitehead Memorial Museum.)

Taini married Erminia Gerola (born of Peitro Gerola and Angelina Pagani on June 11, 1874) on July 15, 1889. Family lore states that John returned to Italy, married, and brought his bride back to Del Rio. The couple had two daughters— Annie, born in 1891, and Lucy, born in 1893.

Taini owned land in South Del Rio; the Qualias were just a short distance away, as were the Bolners, Seraphinis, and others. Taini's town land was on the Creek near the intersection of Pecan and Ney, just north of the Cassinelli Gin House. In fact, Taini gave the City of Del Rio some of his land in order to extend Pecan Street into the southern part of the town. The Cassinellis and Tainis were good friends and at one time lived together in the same dwelling.

Taini was a partner with G.B. Cassinelli in land sales and construction. One record says that the formal partnership began in 1893; other sources state the partnership began in the 1880s. However, a partnership agreement signed 1899 stated "that we G.B. Cassinelli and John Taini of said state and county do by these presents associate ourselves as equal partners under the firm name G.B. Cassinelli and Company to pursue the business of buying, contracting and selling real estate in Lots, Blocks and acres in said state and county with our office in Del Rio." Business was good; the deed records show a great many transactions—on both sides of San Felipe Creek.

The partnership dissolved in 1904. The property division account shows that the firm had been successful. Cassinelli received the "cotton gin & now mill,"

The Joseph Hyman Store on the right is of Taini construction. The building remains in use on the northeast corner of Main and Garfield. The Club Cafe building is further up the block on the left near the roundhouse (in the background). Taini's work is found throughout the heart of Del Rio. (Whitehead Memorial Museum.)

some $540 worth of stone, some $437 worth of brick, a set of school vouchers (although what school construction the company did has yet to be identified), and more. Taini's share of the non-real estate property suggests that he was, at the time, continuing and expanding his career in the construction business: 18 horses and mules, 4 wagons, $354 in bricks, brick-making tools, a mowing machine, plows, a hay press, blacksmith tools, and more. Their substantial tracts of real estate were also divided.

During the late 1880s through the 1910s, John Taini repeatedly won contracts with Val Verde County and the City of Del Rio to build civic improvements. Taini won the contract to repair and enlarge the county jail and to build culverts and bridges. He also laid several miles of pipe and performed the accompanying masonry work to upgrade the water works system bought by the city.

Taini is best known for his many buildings: residential, commercial, theological, and governmental. His earliest work was residential: railroad workers' houses near the railroad reserve, some of the first homes north of the railroad tracks, as well as his own home on South Main Street. He very quickly moved onto the other types of structures, and his work includes many of Del Rio's oldest, most distinctive buildings: the County Courthouse and Jail, Sacred Heart Catholic Church, the old Methodist church building, the Oasis Cafe (one of the few buildings near Brown Plaza to survive the Flood of 1998), the Club Cafe (which was the most popular spot in town for many years), the Hyman Building, and the Warner Building (both on Main Street).

Some of John Taini's earliest known buildings were railroad workers' houses commissioned by the Galveston, Harrisburg & San Antonio (Southern Pacific) Railroad in 1885. This house and another still stand on Martin Street; another is on Broadway.

The Old Methodist Church building on Pecan Street (across from the county courthouse) is one of more than 20 buildings in Del Rio. Many of them, including the courthouse, are still in use. This Taini building's exterior seems to be original, whereas others in use have been substantially altered over the years.

Taini did not neglect the land. Like most of the other Italians, He tilled the land growing vegetables and grapes. John invited his brother Vincenzo (commonly known as Vance) to join him in Del Rio, and in 1911 he did. For 50 years, Vance managed the Taini land and farm interests.

Beyond his business interests, Taini was a leader in the Italian community of Del Rio, although he very rarely forayed into politics. He was an election judge in 1892 and 1894, but such seems to be the extent of it. The bulk of his dealing with the local officials consisted of land transactions for business and affidavits for fellow Italians. For example, upon the death of the Filippones, he testified to the number, age, and location of the heirs for purposes of family inheritance. He was also a member of the Board of Directors and, eventually, one of the last survivors of the Italian Cemetery Association, which had bought land and then given it to the Catholic Church to create what is now part of Sacred Heart Catholic Cemetery.

Taini died in 1929; his wife, Erminia, survived to 1955. The daughters had married and adopted their husbands' names. Their families have since gone from Del Rio, leaving the city with no Tainis except a street in the San Felipe portion of town.

The other Italian settlers are remembered on the maps as well. Cassinelli has a street in San Felipe, while Seraphini, Bolner, Rose, and Qualia all have streets named for them located in South Del Rio—the original Del Rio Italian Colony.

Taini lived in Del Rio from the mid–1880s until his death in 1929. His work crossed into many fields—residential, commercial, theological and civic—in both the predominantly "Anglo" downtown area and the predominantly "Hispanic" San Felipe neighborhood. The John Doak Home on Pecan Street is a wonderful example of Taini's residential work and of the conversion of a historic home to light commercial use.

4. STEEL WHEELS

For many Texas towns, the coming of the railroad was a pivotal event in their histories. In this respect, Del Rio is a typical Texas town. Construction on the line through Val Verde County, eventually called the "Sunset Route," began in the summer of 1881. The Southern Pacific Railroad Company wanted to build a new transcontinental line along a southern route. The distance from San Francisco to the Atlantic Ocean (at New York or Philadelphia) was over 3,000 miles, but a track from San Diego to Galveston would only run 2,100 miles and would give the company a huge competitive edge in shipping costs.

Del Rio's railroad is part of the oldest operating railroad in Texas—the Galveston, Harrisburg & San Antonio. The line first began operation during 1853, though the Civil War interrupted construction. The line opened San Antonio to the Gulf Coast in 1877. Meanwhile, the Southern Pacific had been building line out of its California base during the late 1870s, and by 1881, the track had been laid through the Arizona and New Mexico Territories to El Paso.

The Texas phase of the construction started in San Antonio and El Paso and worked towards the middle, which proved to be a short distance west of the Pecos River. The westward construction proceeded into Val Verde County. The first mile of track out of San Antonio was laid by March 10, 1881; the tracks crossed the Nueces River in December. In that same month the Western Division had laid track east 141 miles out of El Paso to Sierra Blanca. The Western Division's pace of track-laying was slowed by bad weather and lack of supplies.

A narrow railroad bridge was laid across San Felipe Creek on June 22, 1882. The railroad's arrival in Del Rio turned a village into a town. Before the arrival of the railroad, Del Rio's population was just about 200. Shortly afterward, it was almost ten times that, at 1,950. Val Verde County's population soon rose to 2,874, and ten years later in 1900, Val Verde's population had risen to 5,263, most of it in Del Rio. The train tracks, at the time of construction, passed entirely north of the community.

The original railroad depot was at the location of the current depot at Main Street. It was built of lumber with a wide, flat roof, much like old train stations all across Texas. The Southern Pacific (SP) made its stations look even more alike by requiring all of them to be painted yellow with brown trim.

Del Rio first had a wood construction railroad depot. The building in the background to the right appears to be the Club Cafe building, a popular food stop for railroad passengers and crew. (Whitehead Memorial Museum.)

The railroad also built a roundhouse in Del Rio on the north side of the tracks, across from the depot, in what is now an empty, level space used for parking. (A low, curved masonry wall is all that remains of the structure.) It is called a roundhouse because the structure is built around a turntable, which has a short stretch of track on it. A roundhouse is a structure used to house locomotives while they are not being used or while undergoing repairs. To enter the roundhouse, engines were switched off of the main track onto a siding that led to the turntable. Once on it, the turntable operator rotated the turntable to align the engine with the entrance to a stall, and once aligned, the engine backed into the stall.

Originally built in 1883, the roundhouse held 8 engines; a larger replacement building housed 12, although 5 of the stalls were removed as the new diesels were phased into service. The 100-foot diameter turntable, one of the largest on the line, was operated by a man called a hostler. Towards the end of World War II, 1944–1945, the turntable handled 50 engines each day. Next to the roundhouse, the railroad also built two elevated water tanks. The water tanks, one for eastbound trains and one for westbound, were needed because the engines were powered by steam; a fire heated and boiled water into steam, and the steam drove pistons which turned the wheels. Both the roundhouse and tanks were torn down during 1954 after the diesels replaced steam engines.

The railroad company also built Del Rio's first piped water system. Beginning in 1884, the railroad pumped water from San Felipe Creek into a wooden tank, also north of the tracks on the block now known as Star Park. Gravity drew the water through a system of pipes. By 1900, 200 families, besides the railroad employees, were paying $1 per month for this piped-in water. The lot (between

Fourth Street and Fifth Street and between Main Street and Avenue C) was not developed like the neighborhoods around it, probably because most people do not care to live under thousands of gallons of water. The water tank was eventually replaced by the two towers in the Buena Vista area.

A few miles to the northwest lay the Devil's River, and beyond, the Pecos. Between Del Rio and the Devil's River, the railroad followed the Rio Grande. Blasting was required to level parts of the limestone cliffs and to create fill across which the tracks were laid. These rivers and their canyons were the most difficult obstacles to the completion of the railway.

The track immediately west of Del Rio followed the bank of the Rio Grande. Vinton Lee James, a San Antonio resident who frequented the Devil's River Country, recorded his impressions of the area: "The scenery here is truly grand." James continued with descriptions of the "great walls of rock" hanging over the track and the slow speed with which the trains proceeded between cliffs and river.

The work associated with the Devil's River was bridged relatively easily compared to the work needed to bridge the Pecos. In 1882, the Pecos River canyon was the greatest obstacle for railroad engineers and construction crews. A series of detours and special construction projects were needed to accomplish the task of crossing the Pecos River chasm. As the tracks approached the Pecos, from the east and from the west, they turned sharply towards the canyon of Rio Grande, and then went over the cliff-wall into the canyon itself. Long grades had to be blasted off of the cliff-wall to ease the tracks to the floor of the canyon. The 502-foot east tunnel, Tunnel No. 1, was excavated as well. Tunnel No. 2, at 1,425 feet in length, was excavated on the west side of the mouth of the Pecos to raise the tracks back up to the top of the cliffs and out of the canyon. Each tunnel had

During the 1920s, the wooden depot was replaced by the modern brick depot which now houses some City of Del Rio offices. The Del Rio Depot was the first site for many visitors to the city. (Warren Studio.)

39

to blasted out of solid rock. They are the first railroad tunnels in Texas and the only tunnels in the SP's eastern system. The change in elevation from the top of the cliffs to the bottom was 907.27 feet, a significant height when considering the weight of a train being pulled out of the canyon.

The line was completed on January 12, 1883, near a canyon 247 miles from San Antonio and 3 miles west of the Pecos River canyon. The completion was celebrated by the driving of special solid silver spikes into the last wooden crosstie. ("Roy [Bean of Langtry] used to tell how he made a dash after that silver spike as soon as the coast was clear, but a bigger operator than he had got there first. Colonel Pierce [sic] had taken the spike away as a souvenir. Even the redwood tie was cut up into small pieces and distributed among the official guests.") James Campbell, the superintendent of Southern Pacific lines east of El Paso, and James Converse, the chief engineer for the track east of El Paso, alternated strikes on the spike. Thomas Peirce was the highest-ranking official of the railroad present, and he drove in the other spike. Telegraph communications were opened that same day. However, the first trains did not use the track for a few more days. The first westbound train ran on January 25, while the first passenger trains departed New Orleans and San Francisco on February 5, 1883.

The railroad was one of Del Rio's biggest employers and contributors to the city's economy. Del Rio's division headquarters meant office personnel and staff, clerks in the passenger and freight depots, mechanics and smiths, and maintenance crews living and working in the city. Then there were the engineers, firemen, brakemen, and conductors who ran the trains and the additional staff on the passenger trains. Del Rio was very much a railroad town.

This bridge over the Pecos River, flowing southward from the right, at the mouth of the Rio Grande, on the left flowing from the background to the fore, made the southern transcontinental rail line possible. This line was completed in 1883.

The long, winding track from the top of the cliffs down to the level of the bridge (and back up again on the other side) was expensive in time and fuel. That original track was replaced with a more direct line that included the third highest bridge in the world—the Pecos Viaduct, or Pecos High Bridge, completed in 1892.

The Depression of the 1930s hurt rail traffic as it did most other sectors of the economy. Many railroaders were laid off. While some were able to work a few days every six months, to maintain their seniority, many had no work at all. Transients were so common that one railroader saw "as many as sixty hobos in one coal car. There were hundreds and hundreds of them riding the trains." The worst period was that of 1931 to 1934, and though traffic increased during the next two years, it had not yet recovered completely.

Construction projects during 1936 helped get the railroaders employed again. Despite the lower levels of employment, the railroad industry helped carry Del Rio through those years.

While train traffic slacked during the Depression, it boomed during World War II. The mobilization of men and transportation of materials required great numbers of trains in constant operation. Railroad conductor Bonney Vineyard recalled those years:

> Well, [during] World War II, of course, we didn't have near enough men. At one time we thought we had all the trains we could possibly handle. And out of a clear sky, so to speak, an order from the Office of Defense Transportation stating that there would be 300 cars of diesel fuel delivered to the Southern Pacific in Houston by a certain refinery each day for San Diego, California. And it would be, they would expect it to have preferred handling—that in addition to what we thought was all the business we could possibly handle. We handled it; I don't know how.

This bridge once carried trains over the Devil's River. The bridge was actually inside the Devil's River Canyon and had to be destroyed and replaced when Amistad Reservoir flooded the canyon.

The glory days of the railroad are now past, and so is the Southern Pacific. In 1996, the Southern Pacific was bought by the Union Pacific. The Union Pacific Railroad, with its bright yellow and red locomotives, has been expanding dramatically since 1980. In October of that year, the Staggers Act was signed into law deregulating the railroad industry. In 1982, the UP absorbed the Missouri Pacific and the Western Pacific; in 1988, it absorbed the "Katy," the Missouri-Kansas-Texas Railroad; and in 1995, the Chicago & North Western. In 1995, UP attempted to buy the Santa Fe as well but was rebuffed. The Santa Fe merged with the Burlington Northern, and according to UP officials, this action forced the UP to seek acquisition of the SP, a move announced later that year. The UP-SP combination was approved by the U.S. government's Surface Transportation Board on July 3, 1996. The new UP now controls 37,000 miles of track linking 25 American states, Mexico, and Canada. According to UP officials, the buyout was necessary "because we did not have a good route across the southern part of the United States." This explains the SP's archrival UP yellow-and-red locomotives now operating out of Del Rio, the keystone of the old Southern Pacific transcontinental system.

Amtrak still operates the Sunset Limited, stopping in Del Rio and Alpine. However, rumor suggests that Amtrak is planning to reroute the trains. Instead of Houston to San Antonio to El Paso, the Sunset Limited would divert northward to the old Texas & Pacific Railroad line from Houston to Dallas/Fort Worth to El Paso. More recently, news reports from Amtrak officials state that Amtrak may close its cross-country routes entirely in the absence of increased Congressional funding.

Not much freight is brought into or taken out of Del Rio by the railroad in the twenty-first century, but the Union Pacific Railroad still operates out of the old freight depot across Main Street from the passenger depot. The Union Pacific bought the Southern Pacific in 1996.

Private railroad companies, such as the Union Pacific, ended passenger service in the late 1960s and 1970s. The only nationwide passenger rail service now is Amtrak, a government corporation. Many Amtrak trains operate on the East Coast, but few towns in West Texas offer rail service. Between San Antonio and El Paso, the train only stops twice: in Del Rio and Alpine. This photo, dated August 1971, may show the first Amtrak train in Del Rio. (Warren Studio.)

5. The City of Del Rio

The original community name of "San Felipe Del Rio" was a fusion of the names San Felipe Creek and Rio Grande. The name was shortened to "Del Rio" in 1876 with the establishment of a community post office. Local legend states that the United States Post Office Department demanded a different name for the town because the original name was too similar to another Texas town, presumably San Felipe de Austin.

A recommendation was made by H.M. Block, the local postmaster, to change the town's name to avoid confusion with the older East Texas town and the name Del Rio was approved. While "Del Rio" is the name on the map, the part of the town on the east side of San Felipe Creek is still referred to as "San Felipe."

Despite the community's settlement in 1868, the first city government for Del Rio was not organized until 1905. As per state law, Val Verde County Judge J.G. Griner responded to a 141-name petition of "Bona Fide citizens and electors of Del Rio" to hold an election to determine whether a city government would be organized. The petition was submitted on May 16, 1905, and the election was held on May 27. Judge Griner certified that 300 votes were cast, with 182 in favor and 117 opposed. (One lone vote was labeled "Scattering.") The Judge's order then recorded the boundaries and declared the town incorporated.

Two days later, Judge Griner posted in the county courthouse, the post office, and F.C. Blaine's Saloon a notice of election "for the purpose of electing a Mayor, a Marshall and five Aldermen" be to held on June 21, 1905.

The results were tabulated the next day, to wit:

Total number of votes cast:		172
For Mayor:	James McLymont	172
For Marshall:	B.A. Borroum	170
For Aldermen:	J.F. Merritt	171
	E.F. Howard	172
	D.G. Franks	171
	C.A. Jackson	172
	Tom Norvell	172

Del Rio was incorporated in 1905. Dated May 6, this map segment shows the downtown portion of the city. The canals and rail line are also featured prominently, as are the farm tracts in South Del Rio and the western portion of town now known as Chihuahua. (Val Verde County Clerk's Office.)

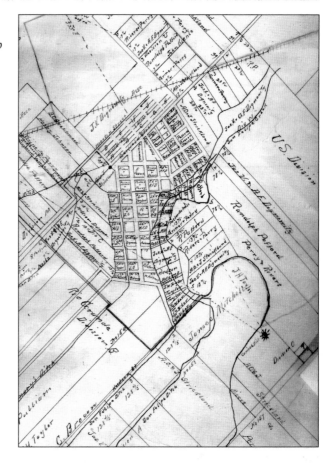

It would seem safe to say that these individuals were probably in league together both for the incorporation of the town and their election.

The first meeting of the board of aldermen occurred on June 30. A boundary survey was the first item of business and then the appointment of various city officials. Attorneys John J. Foster and C.K. McDowell were appointed to draft a city code. The new city government leaned heavily on the existing Val Verde County government. The Precinct 1 justice of the peace was appointed city recorder, and the county attorney was ordered to prosecute violations of the yet-to-be-written city criminal code. Furthermore, this first meeting, and subsequent meetings, took place in the county courthouse.

The city charter included not only the form and style of the government but also a civil and criminal code. A two-thirds vote requirement to assess taxes suggests an intent to limit the city's ability to levy taxes. However, considering the amount of space dedicated to what could be taxed, the code also suggests that taxes were not the same hot button issue they are today. For example, the city taxed real estate, as one might expect, but also specifically taxed livestock, carriages, steam engines, organs and pianofortes, and all other musical instruments, kitchen furniture, jewelry, billiard tables and supplies, sewing machines, and clocks. The code also required each city resident to report all of these things that a person owned. This was not a one-time sales tax on the purchase of such items but a yearly property tax on the possession of such items. The city charged occupation taxes on nearly any job they thought a person might have—attorneys, photographers, bakers, bankers, tailors, dairymen, and even fortune tellers and clairvoyants. The city also taxed events such as theater performances, circuses, cock fights, and fights between bulls and bears.

The criminal code focused on maintaining peace and quiet. This may have been a reaction against the many saloons and other manifestations of "Wild West" life from the town's early years. Horse racing in the streets was prohibited, as was throwing rocks and using slingshots. Vagrancy, public drunkenness, obstructing a sewer or drainage ditch, and swimming nude in San Felipe Creek or in the town's canals were all expressly prohibited. And, of course, merchants were absolutely prohibited from stocking dynamite within the city limits; the city fathers did not want someone to accidentally blow up their town.

The next election was held on August 11, 1906, for mayor and three aldermen. This election was also certified by Judge Griner as per state law. For some unknown reason, the mayor and two aldermen had quit on July 9, eliminating the ability of

Bullfighting is very much a male-dominated profession. However, the sister cities were home to a famous 1950s "Lady Bullfighter": Patricia McCormick. She attended the University of Texas as an art major, but then transferred to Texas Western College to be closer to her true calling in the ring. She participated in her first Fiesta Brava *in 1951 and fought bulls in arenas from Tijuana to Reynosa.*

Del Rio was reincorporated in 1911. This map, dated November 25, 1910, shows the new city limits which were substantially the same as those from the previous incorporation. (Val Verde County Clerk's Office.)

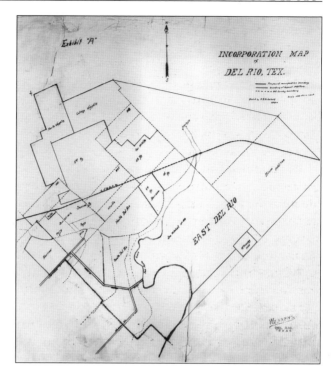

the board of aldermen to form a quorum and conduct city business. The law in such situations required the county judge and commissioners court to call an election to restore the board for the city. They accepted a petition of Del Rio citizens and called for the election. The election was held and the positions filled. (J.W. Newton is a particular mystery in this incident because he was one of the resigning aldermen, a petition signer, and then one of the newly elected aldermen.)

Crisis was averted, but then the board of aldermen minutes simply stop—on October 23, 1906. The minutes resume December 6, 1911, with a different mayor and some different officials, but with no explanation for the lack of recording. (The county's election records also leave a period from 1910 to 1915 unrecorded, so the means by which the new officials won office is a mystery.) The county conducted business during the missing time that would normally be conducted by the city: the creation of a health district, street maintenance, and the like. The records do not say when or how, but at some time after the 1906 election, the city disincorporated. "The Town of Del Rio, in said County, being an unincorporated community" is a phrase in a contract between a telephone company and the county in 1911 and is almost the only positive evidence of the dissolution of the city government. Those records that do exist simply declare election totals for a November 1911 incorporation election. The boundaries of the town were also set forth in the order.

The resumption of records is related to the creation of a new city charter that had been approved November 15, 1911. The record states that the election, once

The city hall, built in 1924, housed the mayor's office and the tax office, as well as the city's fire station, with fire engines in the garage on the left and firefighters living upstairs. (The police station was in a smaller building directly behind city hall.) The men in this photograph are not identified, but surely some Del Rio folks might remember who they are. (Warren Studio.)

again, was ordered, not by the city's mayor or board of aldermen, but by C.K. McDowell, the new Val Verde County judge. This seems to follow Texas law with respect to municipalities, but suggests that the city government had been dismantled: "an incorporation election [may be] called by the county judge on petition of residents of an unincorporated community."

This second city charter in many ways was similar to the first. It included a boundary survey to confirm the city limits and extensive taxation—from nine- and ten-pin alleys and baseball parks to auctioneers, surgeons, and peddlers. The criminal code reflected the mores of the day. The townspeople apparently did not like cussing or other loud, crude language, but they had interesting priorities. Public drunkenness brought a $100 fine; blocking a sidewalk brought a $50 fine. Vagrancy earned a punishment of $200. Beating a dog was fineable by $50, but beating a person—assault and battery—could only be punished with a fine of $25.

The new charter also decreased the size of the city council. The governing body included the mayor and only two councilmen, called commissioners, and the body was known as the city commission. The record of the county commissioners shows 164 votes "For Commission" and 140 "Against Commission." George McMullen was elected mayor, and J.O. Taylor and G.M. Atkinson were elected commissioners. No actual totals were recorded; the men were said to have all been elected with pluralities.

This government continued for seven years, handling the day-to-day business of the small, but growing, metropolitan area of more than 10,000 inhabitants.

Sidewalk construction and maintenance were very important, and property owners were ordered to build sidewalks under threat of fines and liens. Del Rio also adopted a lengthy dairy ordinance and began installation of electric streetlights.

The threat of smallpox at the turn of the century prompted the city commission to make the medical health inspector a powerful and highly paid individual. Another county site, though one that has been lost, was an old smallpox quarantine camp. The county commissioners court employed someone to visit the camp each week and report back to the court. The court did have someone on salary; "a man was allowed $30.50 for guarding and extra work" at the camp, which was located in the southeast section of Del Rio across San Felipe Creek. Smallpox was also the reason for temporarily cutting ties with the nearby towns in Mexico. The following was reported:

> From January 30, 1891, until April 1, 1891, Val Verde County was quarantined against the towns of Las Vacas [now Ciudad Acuña] and Himenes [Jiminez]. The quarantine order was to be published in the *Del Rio Record* and in *El Fraternal*, a Mexican paper published in Del Rio; and the proclamation was to be distributed in the Mexican towns.

Smallpox remained a threat in the early twentieth century. During February 1909, smallpox vaccinations were ordered by the county commissioners for all students in public and private schools. Once the City of Del Rio was reincorporated, the county and city jointly purchased the "smallpox camp in East

The new city hall was constructed on Broadway in 1960, as it is shown here. The building has been enlarged and remodeled since that time. (Warren Studio.)

Del Rio, between the Eagle Pass road and the East Side Water Company tank. About 10 acres of ground was [*sic*] purchased for this purpose."

During the World War I years, the Texas State Legislature passed laws allowing cities of sufficient size (10,000 people, but later 5,000) to organize themselves under charters adopted by the inhabitants of the city. The City of Roses took advantage of this law and adopted its third city charter in 1918, its first home rule charter.

The work towards Del Rio's home rule charter actually began in 1917. A citizens' committee was proposed on July 24th and elected to proceed that October. On March 18, 1918, the proposed charter was presented to the city commission, and it was adopted by the voters of Del Rio on May 10, 1918.

The new charter was much longer than the previous charters and is much more recognizable as a governing document in contrast with the earlier charters. Most of the criminal code placed in ordinances by the previous charters were condensed into a single section without getting into the specifics of definitions and exact fines but stating that the city government has power to regulate or prohibit certain activities. The World War I years also saw nighttime curfews.

The major issues addressed in the 1918 Charter were public utilities, civic improvements, and deficit financing. These issues repeatedly emerged during the next decades as the city bought waterworks plants and water distribution systems, installed sanitary sewers, and paved streets—and paid for these with bonds, sometimes not redeemable for 25 or 30 years. Another issue particularly dealt with in the charter was taxicabs, or as they were identified—hacks, drays, and

This Noah Rose photograph shows wooden buildings just one block east of Main Street on Pecan and Martin Streets. Most photographs of early Del Rio show Main Street and the brick and masonry construction of the commercial buildings. In those same years (c. 1912) most Del Rio buildings were constructed of wood or adobe. (Whitehead Memorial Museum.)

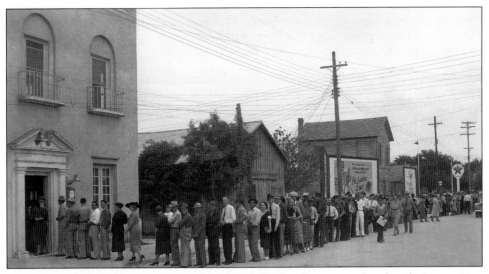

The old city hall building was vacated in the 1960s, but it was not abandoned. At one time, it was the Boys and Girls Club headquarters and, more recently, it has been the home of the Del Rio Council for the Arts. This photo seems to show Del Rio residents lined up to vote. The building to the right (east) of City Hall has been replaced with Humphrey's Gun Shop. The buildings beyond it are part of Eagle Pass Lumber Company, which was demolished to make way for the new federal courthouse. (Warren Studio.)

drivers of baggage wagons. Four paragraphs were dedicated to the matter, and for years afterward the city commission passed ordinances on the matter.

The city's governing body was called a city commission as in the previous government. It also included a mayor and two commissioners, all serving two-year terms and all being elected at-large. The office requirements reflect the much more strict suffrage requirements of the day. The mayor had to be a United States citizen and qualified voter, and he had to be a Del Rio resident for a year and a "bona fide owner of real estate in the City for at least two years." The commissioners had to be U.S. citizens and qualified voters; they had to meet the one-year residency requirement and be an owner of property in the city.

Voters for officer elections had to be at least 21 years of age, "entitled to vote for members of the State Legislature," and six-month residents within the city limits. However, people wanting to vote in bond elections also had to be "qualified voters who are property tax payers within the City."

The 1918 City Charter was amended only twice—in 1935 and again in 1953. The 1935 charter revision came about due to confusion about the city's boundaries. On October 11, 1921, the city commission had deannexed territory that was uninhabited, unplatted, and used exclusively for agriculture. Del Rio was by then acknowledged as the "Wool and Mohair Capital of the World" due to the extensive presence of sheep and goat ranching. Del Rio was (and remains) surrounded by agricultural land. According to the ordinance, the lands were included within the

Del Rio corporate boundaries "by mistake." The ordinance was passed, and the land was taken off the city tax rolls, and the matter seemed to end there.

However, the matter returned to the commission on May 8, 1934, in the form of an outside attorney's letter explaining that the city charter did not allow for deannexation of territory. He declared that state law governing cities states, "A municipal Corporation can not disconnect territory which has been legally annexed by an Ordinance purporting to define its boundairies [sic]."

The city attorney rejected the interpretation. A series of arguments on both sides was presented. The relevant section of the charter "provide[d] for the extension of said limits of said City, and the annexation of additional territory lying adjacent to said City," but did not specify the power of removal of territory from the city.

The issue was resolved the next year. The commission passed an ordinance on January 23rd calling for an election on two proposals to amend the charter: adoption of the deannexed boundary and deletion of the city charter's Section 23A about the board of managers for the waterworks. Second and third readings were passed in subsequent meetings, and the matter was put before the people on March 23, 1935. Both measures passed overwhelmingly, and the measures were declared adopted at the April 2nd canvassing. What apparently had been a huge ruckus was settled quite handily, and the issue was put to rest.

A second attempt to amend the city charter came about in 1950. The slate of amendment proposals would have expanded the city council to a mayor and five

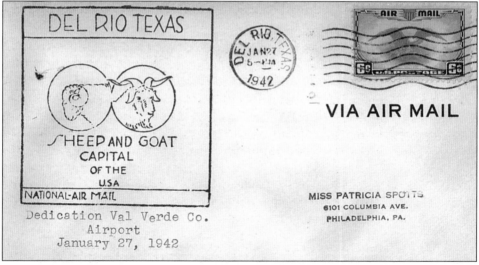

Most of the county is rural in nature, and ranching was and remains much more common. Cattle grazed the countryside during the late 1800s and early 1900s. However, the dry range and brushy undergrowth supports sheep and goats more easily than cattle and horses. Del Rio was the center of sheep and goat country and became known as the "Wool and Mohair Capital of Texas," "of the United States," and even "of the World."

MAIN STREET, DEL RIO, TEXAS—7

The sender wrote on the back of this postcard that he had a good time in Del Rio and Villa Acuña. Several of the buildings shown in this 1930s postcard are recognizable today.

members with each member elected from one of five wards. No at-large seats other than the mayor would be allowed. The proposals were voted down, but this presaged a move a decade later to expand and modernize the city government.

The second successful charter amendment proposal came about in 1953. Since the 1920s, the Citizens Bridge Company had owned and operated the Del Rio–Villa Acuña International Bridge. In 1953, the company announced that it was going to put the bridge up for sale. The city charter carried no provisions for operating such an enterprise; nevertheless, city ownership of the bridge and the authority to charge tolls were considered to be beneficial for the city's future. The election ordinance was quite lengthy, but on October 9, 1953, the voters approved the necessary amendments, and the city took possession of the bridge properties. The bridge has proven, and continues to be, economically fruitful for the City coffers.

The failure to expand the size of the city commission in 1950 did not end interest in doing so or in changing the form of city government. The city council approved an ordinance on November 23, 1965, calling for an election for a new city charter. The ballot came with two questions, the first being "SHALL A COMMISSION BE CHOSEN TO FRAME A NEW CHARTER?" The voting on this question was designed strangely. A voter had to mark out the word "NO" to indicate a yes vote, and vice versa. The second part listed a number of prominent citizens who could be elected to the charter commission. The ballot also allowed for write-in names. The second reading passed on December 7, and the third on December 14. The vote carried solidly with

269 in favor and 93 opposed. All of the proposed commission members were approved with negligible write-in votes cast.

The charter commission returned to council on March 20, 1967 with a proposal. Council approved it unanimously and ordered the charter election for May 27, 1967. Six thousand copies were printed for the public.

The key change in the proposal was a conversion from the "commission" form of city government to a "council-manager" form. This would have at least three major policy implications. First, the power of the mayor would be greatly diminished. Second, the mayor and council members would no longer have direct authority over the day-to-day operations of the city departments. Third, the council would be expanded from a total of three members all elected at-large to a total of seven, with three elected from specific districts. This would allow more people to sit in charge of policy-making for the city and allow neighborhoods to promote their interests. This (in conjunction with national trends such as the elimination of the poll tax) offered more opportunities for Hispanics to win elective office. (None of the mayors and only a tiny number of commissioners had been Hispanic up to this time.)

The election resulted in a strange mix of support and rejection. Precinct 1 included the old part of Del Rio including Main Street, most of the business district, and all of the land west of San Felipe Creek and south of the railroad tracks. Precinct 2 was all the territory north of the railroad tracks. Precinct 3 was the San Felipe neighborhoods east of the Creek. Precinct 1 voted two-to-one in favor at 631-350. Precinct 2 voted overwhelmingly in favor at 921-181. The

The 1960s are now history. This southern portion of the commercial district included the Texas Theater and Beall's on the west side of the street and Montgomery Ward and Calderon Pharmacy on the east.

predominantly Hispanic Precinct 3 voted overwhelmingly against: 80 for but 1,039 opposed. Overall, the vote totaled 1,632 in favor and 1,570 against.

On the day the votes were canvassed, May 31, the city commission became a city council and shortly thereafter City Secretary E.W. Marlowe was hired as city manager. The current members of the commission remained in office but were redesignated councilmen serving as an interim council until elections could be organized.

The new charter continued the property ownership requirements and effectively stiffened that clause by requiring the mayor and council members to meet the property ownership requirement for two years. Residency requirements were also increased to two years for all seven members. The position of mayor, however, was greatly reduced in power; the mayor held ceremonial powers but "no regular administrative duties." Essentially, the administrative powers were transferred to the city manager, who had the power to hire and fire city staff. The manager could be from anywhere, but during his tenure of office, he was required to reside within the city limits.

The ordinance calling for the first election under the adopted charter was not called until January 9, 1968. The mayor and council members Place A, Place B, and Place C were to be elected at-large, while council members District 1, District 2, and District 3 were to be elected by the voters in those three voting precincts. The specifics of the election were established at the next meeting on January 22.

The election was held on April 2, and 4,858 votes were canvassed. Dr. Alfredo Gutierrez was elected mayor, the city's first Hispanic in that position, and four other people won clean majorities in their races. The District 2 and District 3 elections each had three-way splits and required run-off elections. Those were held and the winners were seated May 14, 1968, and the complete new city council was in place.

The three districts initially followed the traditional Del Rio precinct boundaries without regard to population. A series of United States Supreme Court decisions during the 1960s forced a change in this policy. The charter defined the old district boundaries but also stated that council should make adjustments in the boundaries to keep the populations of the three districts roughly equal. As the city's population has grown, this requirement has pulled the two districts from south of the railroad tracks northward.

Another development found in the charter is a throwback to old, small-town government. The charter allows for "qualified voters" to propose legislation under the power of initiative, and it also allows for referendum. The most interesting thing, however, is that "The mayor or any other member of the city council may be removed from office by recall." Political fights have on several occasions become intense. One mayor has been removed from office. Another mayor and a number of council members have also faced recall challenges. The recall rules have in some ways made city politics more participatory but also more contentious.

The charter also gave the city a power it had never had before—extraterritorial jurisdiction extending 5 miles beyond the city limits. Annexation had been

President McKinley's first stop on the Mexican border—at Del Rio, Texas.
Copyright 1901 by Underwood & Underwood.

Del Rio is known as the "City of Presidents" because of three presidential visits in the 1960s associated with Amistad Dam. However, Del Rio has been visited by several other Presidents of the United States because of its southern cross-country railroad, including Benjamin Harrison (1891), William McKinley (shown here in a 1901 stereo card), William Howard Taft (1909), Calvin Coolidge (1930), and Harry Truman (1948).

relatively rare before World War II. Since that time, developers have repeatedly petitioned the city for annexation, which has been done. The annexations and the extraterritorial jurisdiction, the increasing population of the city, and the exodus of rural population to the city have combined to create a situation where the city government has regulatory authority over the vast majority of Val Verde residents.

Over the years Del Rio has had many identities—identities expressed in the form of nicknames. One of them is "the City of Roses." The name was in use early in the early twentieth century. Many of the Del Rio Civic League's early projects were "clean town campaigns." This group appears to have been part of the Progressive movement popular in Texas in the first two decades. They sponsored "tree planting, uniform parking of streets, and beautiful, cultured home environments." The league established parks, swimming pools, and other "wholesome" diversions. Del Rio became noted for its "riotous growth of flowers." The abundance of flowers, particularly its roses, led to the town nickname. "The roses never bloom out black / In Del Rio; The sun has never shown its back / To Del Rio." As one early Del Rio resident penned (rather floridly), "nature gave our soil every element that goes to make it a natural home for flowers. That is why we are called the 'City of Roses,' our strawberry the delightful flavor and the peach the beautiful blush."

A second nickname sometimes used is "the City of Presidents." Five American presidents have visited the city by rail. Three presidents came to Del Rio (and Ciudad Acuña) in relation to the Amistad project. Dwight Eisenhower, Lyndon Baines Johnson, and Richard Nixon each flew into Laughlin A.F.B. and met the

The growing urban community of Del Rio has always stayed close to the rugged canyon country in the rural areas of Val Verde County.

crowds while meeting with his counterpart from Mexico either in town or at the dam site. Two other men visited Del Rio and later became President of the United States: George Bush, during the Amistad dedication, and Governor George W. Bush, during the cleanup efforts following the Flood of 1998.

Another nickname for Del Rio is "the Queen City of the Rio Grande," a name in use as early as the 1920s. The name's origin, however, seems to have been lost. Some speculation has been along the lines of Del Rio's former status as the second largest city on the Rio Grande, El Paso being the largest. Though no longer the case, historically, Del Rio has been larger than Laredo or any of the towns in the Rio Grande Valley.

The name was popularized in more recent times by a local sportswriter named Carl Guys. Guys had grown up in "the Windy City" (Chicago) and "the Queen of the Western Suburbs" (Hinsdale, Illinois). When he began writing for the *News-Herald* around 1950, Del Rio had no nickname in use. Travelling to away games of the local schools' athletic teams, Guys discovered that most towns in the area did use some kind of nickname, and he thought Del Rio should have one as well. Ultimately, he began using "Queen City" in his sports column, and the moniker stuck.

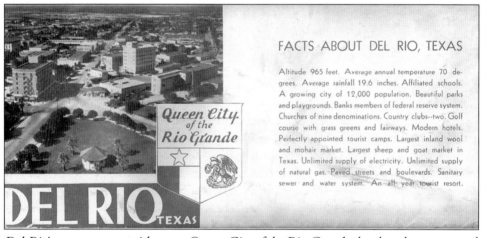

Del Rio's most common nickname, Queen City of the Rio Grande, has long been promoted by Del Rio's chamber of commerce. This pamphlet dates to the 1930s.

6. A COUNTY FOR THE COUNTY SEAT

The legal organization of Val Verde County occurred in 1885—after the area was settled but before the city's incorporation. The county was formed from parts of three counties: Kinney to the east, Crockett to the north, and Pecos to the west. The borders of Val Verde County encompassed 3,150 square miles, more ground than the states of Rhode Island (776) and Delaware (1,309) combined, or nearly the size of Connecticut (3,212). It was the sixth largest county in Texas at the time (though it is now seventh).

The formation of the county is directly linked to the coming of the railroad and the dramatic growth of Del Rio in the years following. Before the railroad, Del Rio was a small town on the western fringe of Kinney County. By coming to Del Rio, the railroad gave the town a huge boost in economic activity and population growth. And because the railroad bypassed the county seat of Brackettville, that town did not keep pace, and Del Rio quickly outgrew it. As a result, there was growing popular demand for the creation of a new county with Del Rio as the county seat.

The territory of Val Verde County has existed within several different jurisdictional boundaries. In 1836, the land now in Val Verde was assigned to Bexar County with San Antonio as the county seat; essentially, all of Texas west of San Antonio lay within this district. Throughout the years of the Republic, no changes occurred. In 1850, several new counties were established by the state legislature. Presidio County (named for the Spanish fort near modern Presidio) and El Paso County were organized west of the Pecos, with Presidio County in possession of the future Langtry area. Uvalde and Kinney Counties were created in that same year. Kinney County's boundaries lay much farther south than they do now, encompassing the vicinities of Quemado and Eagle Pass, and bordering Webb County near Laredo. All of the Val Verde area east of the Pecos, including Del Rio, still lay within the Bexar County Land District. When Maverick County was created in 1856 from parts of Webb and Kinney Counties, Kinney County was recompensed with extra lands to the north, including the southeastern parts of Val Verde along the Sycamore and across the lowest reaches of the Devil's River. In 1858, Dawson County was created from parts of Kinney and Uvalde Counties, but the county was never actually organized. It remained on the maps for eight years, but it finally disappeared by 1866, when boundary line changes for Uvalde,

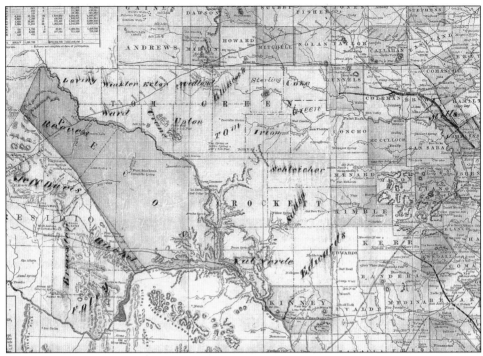

This map shows southwest Texas, Del Rio's neighbors, and the creation of Val Verde County. (Texas General Land Office.)

Kinney, and Maverick Counties effectively erased the phantom county. Val Verde County probably owes its existence to this erasure.

The origin of Val Verde County's name is the subject of some debate. At least as early as 1882, the San Antonio *Weekly Express* referred to Del Rio as being in "Val Verde County" even though no such legal entity yet existed. "Val Verde" is a pair of Spanish words that translate as "green valley," an apt description of the immediate surroundings of San Felipe Creek. However, "Val Verde" is also the name of a site in central New Mexico along the Rio Grande where a small battle was fought during the Mexican War and a better known battle was fought during the American Civil War. That Battle of Val Verde was a victory for the Confederate and Texas troops in early spring of 1862.

The county could have been named "Peirce." A group of local business owners were interested in that name for the county because of an offer by Thomas W. Peirce, formerly in charge of the Galveston, Harrisburg & San Antonio Railroad. When that railroad was absorbed into the Southern Pacific system, he became a vice-president in the larger company. However, "he found that he could do nothing without consulting his superior." Having lost power in the company, he sought to immortalize his name on the map of Texas, promising to build a good hospital in Del Rio if the new county were named for him. The group, called the "Ice House Clique," was the first group to go to Austin on behalf of the proposed county, but this early effort failed to convince the Texas Legislature to approve the county's formation.

Following the initial defeat, Judge W.K. Jones, a Dr. Nicholson, and a Mr. Varney became Del Rio's point-men at the state capital. The three went to Austin in 1885 to lobby in person for the organization of Val Verde County. The great size of Kinney County, the population of the proposed county being greater than the legal requirements, as well as the public interest were their arguments. They were successful; upon reconsideration on March 24 of that year, House Bill 105, the organic law for Val Verde, was passed. On May 2, the county was organized and officials were elected. No records are extant telling exactly what happened to change the minds of the legislators, but something important must have been said.

There is a tradition in Texas and in the rest of the South of dedicating and naming things for Confederate Civil War figures. At least one obvious example can be easily found in Val Verde County. On the grounds of the county courthouse, under a tree at the northwest corner of courthouse square, stands a pink granite monument. The final part of the inscription reads, "A Memorial to Texans who served the Confederacy."

The name origins of several neighboring counties merit particular notice. Terrell County bordering Val Verde on the west is named for Confederate General Alexander Watkins Terrell. Sutton County on Val Verde's northern boundary is named for Confederate Lieutenant Colonel John Schuler Sutton, who died of his battle injuries sustained during the Battle of Val Verde in New Mexico. Schleicher

The county courthouse, as it was originally built, included the center tower and four conical turrets. The statues above the door disappeared years ago and, despite some searching, have not been found. (Whitehead Memorial Museum.)

County on Sutton's northern border is named for Confederate Captain Gustav Schleicher. And, Tom Green County on Schleicher's northern border is named for Confederate General Thomas Green, who is credited in some works with the Confederate victory in the Battle of Val Verde.

With this pattern in mind, it seems reasonable that Val Verde County was named for the battlesite. This belief is supported by a number of local and state sources, including the county historical marker in Moore Park along San Felipe Creek. The marker states, "Val Verde County . . . Named in Honor of the Battle Fought at Val Verde, near Fort Craig, New Mexico."

Detractors have a point, however, when they state that, to date, no documentary material has surfaced to confirm this theory. It is far easier to state that "Val Verde" is nothing more than an environmental observation. Specifically, early Del Rioan Randolph Pafford is credited for naming the area Val Verde. The idea of "green valley" is all the more plausible when understood that some of the English-speaking settlers had Spanish-speaking wives. Furthermore, A.F. Dignowity, one of the key men involved in creating the county, was a Union veteran of the Civil War. Therefore, it would not be logical for him to commemorate the Confederate victory.

On the other hand, H.M. Block, one of the earliest settlers and community leaders (and postmaster for whom the city's name is credited), was a Civil War Confederate veteran. He had even served with Sibley's Brigade, which fought in the New Mexico campaign. He married in San Antonio in 1864, then served with Colonel John S. "Rip" Ford at the close of the war. In 1874, he arrived in San Felipe Del Rio, went into partnership with James Taylor, then bought out Taylor's share from his wife, Paula, after Taylor died. He served in several government capacities before dying in 1932 at the age of 90. It seems that such a prominent figure could easily have influenced the naming of the county. And while it seems odd to think that a Union Civil War veteran would support the naming of the county for a Confederate victory, it seems just as odd for a bunch of post-Reconstruction Texas Democrats to support and name two streets for a Civil War Union army veteran. The Democrats of the "Dignowity Clique" would not support Dignowity, "a staunch Republican," unless he was willing to give them something—something better than a new hospital. There must have been a deal, and Val Verde County was placed on the map of Texas.

The organic act provided details for the formation of the new county. The Kinney County Commissioners Court was authorized to draw the precinct boundaries within Val Verde and provide for the election of county officers. A portion of the debts of the three counties was assumed by the new county government. The county was assigned to the 27th Senate District and the 81st House District for representation in the Texas Legislature. Val Verde was placed in the 11th U.S. Congressional district for the state. An emergency clause was attached to the bill allowing for the bill to take effect immediately upon passage.

May 18, 1885 may be considered the founding date of Val Verde County. On that date, the first county commissioners court meeting was held. Presiding was

From right to left are Henry Mills, Tuff Whitehead, and Alicemae Fitzpatrick, one of the first female county officials and the person for whom the courthouse annex is named. Fitzpatrick served as assistant county clerk and as county clerk for more than 50 years combined. The remaining men are Clarence Hereford, Tom Brite, and Mr. Love. (Warren Studio.)

Judge W.K. Jones; attending the meeting were Commissioners John Glynn and W.H. Liles, Sheriff W.H. Jones, and County Clerk Peter Porter. Government being what it is, the county immediately got to work on taxes, naming a tax assessor, and requesting lists of delinquent taxpayers from the three parent counties. The commissioners court also appointed a committee to "ascertain the probable costs of running a county here" and to "see whether the money could be borrowed on the credit of the county at a reasonable rate of interest."

The court also named a constable and some justices of the peace. Having these officials, the county also needed a courthouse, for which it rented from Randolph Pafford a stone building opposite the Del Rio Hotel for $20 per month. Also, a "store building" owned by B.C. Greenwood was rented at $10 per month for use as a jail. The county judge and commissioners paid themselves $3 for three days of commissioners' court work and paid the sheriff two dollars for the same.

The map of the county drawn by the Kinney County commissioners' court was accepted as drawn. On June 11, 1885 the county clerk was ordered to correspond with the Kinney County judge concerning the organization of Val Verde County and to notify the Texas secretary of state that Val Verde County was then organized and operational. Apparently the map contained some errors because shortly thereafter the commissioners court had Archibald Bogle, who was serving as county surveyor, make a map of that portion of Val Verde County west of the Pecos. He was paid $5.55 for the job.

The formation of the county necessitated the building of a county courthouse. On July 11, 1887, the county commissioners court adopted the site for the courthouse, and that fall let a contract for $32,500. The architectural firm of Larmour and Watson (from Austin) designed the building. The courthouse was completed in 1888. The firm of Hood and McLeod won the overall construction contract, but John Taini, who had built many of the stone structures at Fort Clark and several homes in Del Rio, was sub-contracted for the stonework. Local legend says that much of the work was actually done by former Chinese railroad laborers, out of work after the completion of the Southern Pacific Railroad. The courthouse was enlarged and remodeled in 1915 by San Antonio architect Atlee Ayres at a cost of $27,500. Much of the ornamentation was removed, and a third floor was added.

The county courthouse, however, had fallen on hard times by 1995. The Texas Historical Commission labeled the courthouse as one of "Texas' top 10 most-endangered properties" for the year. Commission architect Stan Graves visited the courthouse, which he called "fabulous," and concluded that it was in danger and that the citizens of the county should be concerned. Graves added, however, that "it's not time to panic just yet."

Time to panic happened that May. May 5 was the 25th anniversary of District Judge George Thurmond's tenure on the bench. On that same day, large pieces of plaster fell out of the ceiling into the court secretary's office. No one was injured, though there was much noise and a great deal of dust. Some courthouse work was suspended pending an inspection; "crumblings" were heard in other parts of the building, so the second and third floors were closed entirely. The

The courthouse was greatly modified in 1915. A third floor was added and much of the ornamental roofing was removed. (Whitehead Memorial Museum.)

architect inspecting the building said that "the metal roof of the courthouse [was] supporting the rafters instead of the rafters supporting the roof." An evacuation of the building was ordered.

Val Verde County may be the only county in Texas in possession of two functioning historic courthouses. After the closure of the county courthouse, a deal was struck between the federal government and Val Verde County giving the county the Old Federal Courthouse on Main Street. Initially, County Judge Ray Kirkpatrick signed the agreement with the General Services Administration (GSA) to use the building temporarily, at no charge to the county other than upkeep, pending its disposal by the federal government. The federal government had moved into a new modern facility across Broadway and down the block but had yet to sell the Old Federal Building, though sealed bids were being taken through May 25 of the same year. The Old Federal Building had been vacant the whole time since the federal government moved in the early 1990s.

County business resumed as the move of the various offices was completed. Some offices were moved in mid-May, but the last office was not until the last of the month. The County appropriated $20,000 for the move. The federal building was in good shape structurally, though new paint was needed.

Some uncertainty about the situation existed. The Old Federal Building was scheduled to be sold. The GSA realty officer, Jerry Moore, said that the county would have first priority for purchase but that he was not certain about the county's intentions. County Judge Kirkpatrick said that he did not want to abandon the Val Verde County Courthouse, yet it clearly was not in shape for use. Scaffolding had been put up in many of the rooms to hold the ceilings up. (Removing the law library from its third floor home eliminated a great deal of weight stress.) Architect Kim Williams noted the structural failure in one of the four roof beams, code violations, dry rot, and more. With no possibility of moving back in the very near future, the county announced its intention to acquire the federal building, and the impending sale was canceled. Through the intervention of Congressional officials, the GSA then gave the building to the county.

Meanwhile, County Judge Ray Kirkpatrick began a plan to restore the county courthouse building. Roof beams were replaced, and the roof steadied. Stonework was done, though this work is a slow, laborious process. Each bad stone in the courthouse walls has to be chipped out and removed by hand. Then, each replacement stone must be cut to fit and mortared into the gap—one at a time. The interior of the building was nearly gutted for a new climate control system and the wiring necessary for modern governmental functions: telephone, electrical, and computer network. (An earlier book, *Val Verde County*, has several photographs of the restoration work in progress.)

Many county offices returned to the reconditioned county courthouse, though some stayed in the Old Federal Building along with the state district court, and both buildings remain in use. On courthouse square work is ongoing. The county just received another $2.5 million from the state to continue with stonework and other elements of restoration.

7. Soldiers of the Frontier

The word "frontier" encompasses a great many ideas. In traditional American history, "the Frontier" was a geographic region—the vast unknown, uncharted, or uninhabited land beyond the line of settlement. "Frontier" may also reflect a more European idea represented in the Spanish *frontera*. *La frontera* is a political boundary between two countries; it is "the Border." The United States Army has on two occasions established posts in and near Del Rio for reasons associated with both definitions.

On September 6, 1876, Camp San Felipe was established and garrisoned by troops stationed at Fort Clark. It seems, however, that while this was the first permanent post in Del Rio, the army had used land near the townsite for a temporary post as early as 1856 or 1857. It was probably a semi-regular field camp for soldiers from Fort Clark. There is mention of Federal troops being removed from the post in 1861 and a reoccupation in 1866. These are the same dates for the closing and reopening of Fort Clark, and they reflect the relationship between the two posts. The land for the permanent post was deeded by the irrigation company in 1877 and construction began in 1880. Camp San Felipe was located on 400 acres along the east bank of San Felipe Creek about half of a mile from the springs, and the army had permission to use another 1,476 acres if needed.

In the earlier years of operation, the post was known as "Camp San Felipe," but when the name of the town changed, "Camp Del Rio" came into common usage and became official on March 18, 1881. The declared purpose of the permanent camp was to prevent "Mexican Indians" from stealing and running horses along the Rio Grande near the mouths of the Devil's and the Pecos Rivers. Many West Texas towns reported raids from Comanche, Kickapoo, and Lipan Apache groups from Mexico, particularly the area around Rey Molino, and from the Indian Territory north of the Red River.

Post buildings included an eclectic mix of adobe, plank wood, stone and wood construction, and tents. The permanent structures had roofs of cypress shingles freighted in from Helena in Karnes County. Generally, cut lumber was freighted to Val Verde through San Antonio in oxcarts. The main post was not at the water's edge, but located on a plateau above the springs. The post was considered by the soldiers preferable to Fort Duncan at Eagle Pass because of the better health conditions for the soldiers and the social activities provided in nearby San Felipe Del Rio. The post closed during 1891, but title was not transferred from the army back to the irrigation company until May 19, 1896. While the post was officially closed, "troops continued to serve at Del Rio as needed." Parenthetically, Eagle Pass also had an army post at this time called Camp Eagle Pass, "a sub-post of Fort Clark," as was Camp Del Rio. That post was also "closed" in 1891, though troops remained for some years afterward.

In the 1970s, the city council was presented with a proposal to rebuild the post in the interests of attracting tourists along with historic preservation. The council was planning on developing some property at or near the site of the post, but the Val Verde County Historical Commission suggested that the development might destroy the site. The city manager pointed out that a survey of the area had been done in the early 1970s and that no evidence of Camp Del Rio had been found. Nevertheless, no action to rebuild was ever taken.

The post had been constructed on the banks of the San Felipe Creek for obvious reasons. During the preparations for America's 200th anniversary celebrations in 1976, several parks were built alongside San Felipe Creek. Several thousand feet of walkways were laid and benches set. Some of the banks of the creek were walled with rock. Recreational sites were incorporated into the plan: the amphitheater was carved into a hillside, and courts for volleyball, tennis, and basketball opened. Much of this construction is on the grounds of old Camp Del Rio.

A long standing local legend states that the numbers of troops at Camp Michie increased so quickly that many of them lived in tents or other temporary shelters. The name Michie is commonly misspelled. (Whitehead Memorial Museum.)

Del Rio was also home to a second United States Army post, a World War I–era post named Camp Michie. One of the few written records about the post notes the following: "Del Rio, Tex., Camp U.S. Troops: Semi-permanent camp, located on outskirts of Del Rio, Valverde [*sic*] County. Established incidental to border patrol activities during Mexican Revolution, 1911–1920. Cantonment for one regiment of cavalry constructed, 1918; salvaged 1919. Headquarters, Del Rio District, Mexican Border Patrol."

Extant documentation is sparse, but does include the origin of the post's name:

> War Department records show that a camp at Del Rio Texas, was constructed to accommodate a regiment of cavalry during 1917–1918. The camp was named Camp Robert E.L. Michie in honor of Brigadier General Robert E.L. Michie who died in France on June 4, 1918, by Section I, Paragraph 1, of General Orders No. 38, War Department, Washington, dated June 24, 1920. General Michie served as Adjutant of the 12th Cavalry during 1901–1903, at Fort Clark, Texas." The post was established as a result of the "frequent raids upon border towns from Mexican revolutionists.

Apparently, the soldiers were required to raise the tents themselves. (Val verde County Historical Commission.)

While a much greater portion of Camp Michie lay on the east side of the creek, some of the soldiers were housed in the area between Roosevelt Park and San Felipe Creek in an area called Ramageville. This photo shows some of those living quarters at Ramageville. (Val Verde County Historical Commission.)

The first unit at the camp was the U.S. 14th Cavalry. The troops had the duty of protecting the border and the railroad bridges up to Langtry, including the key bridge at the Pecos.

The second decade of the twentieth century saw the Revolution in Mexico and the Great War in Europe. The general military buildup to prepare soldiers for overseas deployment and the concern about United States–Mexican border security prompted the army to station several military units in Val Verde. The camp was organized quickly and certainly without proper planning for logistics; an early camp commander, Major Treadwell, and his wife lived in Del Rio because there were no quarters for them on the post. Other soldiers were housed in tents due to a shortage of wooden buildings; nevertheless, there were enough soldiers to have a marching band. The hospital, one of the few permanent structures because of its importance, was located in the vicinity of the intersection of Gibbs Street and Bedell Avenue, very near where U.S. 90 crosses San Felipe Creek. As many as four regiments trained at Camp Michie. Two of the cavalry regiments, the 307th and 313th, were organized here. The 12th Cavalry was also known to operate at Michie. Some of the men stationed at Camp Michie were later deployed to El Paso and assigned to General "Blackjack" Pershing's command and sent into Mexico after Pancho Villa.

One of the most important jobs of the military was the guarding of the Pecos High Bridge. Because the railroad linked ports on the Pacific Ocean with those on the Gulf of Mexico, the rail line became a vital link in moving men and munitions around the country. The bridge had to be protected. During the war, U.S. Army soldiers, assisted by Texas Rangers, were stationed on the Pecos River to prevent sabotage of the High Bridge. The government actually began patrolling around the High Bridge several years before 1914, "when trouble along the Mexican border resulted in a battalion of coast artillerymen being moved in to protect the structure."

Very little documentation remains of Camp Michie. The U.S. 5th Cavalry occupied the post in 1921 (and perhaps the very first part of 1922). This unit appears to have been the last military occupation of Camp Michie at Del Rio:

> On March 28, 1923, the Secretary of War by endorsement to the Quartermaster General declared Camp Robert E.L. Michie, Del Rio, Texas, surplus and directed the Quartermaster General to take "proper

The Martin family lived, worked, and fished on the Devil's River. Records from the 1850s through the 1960s indicate that the rivers near Del Rio have long been the favorites of fishermen. (Dudley Martin and Daisy Speer.)

steps looking to the disposal of the buildings, utilities, and lands, law and regulations governing."

With the exception of some buildings used by the Del Rio Country Club, landmarks were difficult to find, and they are all but gone now. Apparently, those "proper steps" of disposal cleared most of the site rather effectively.

The Pecos High Bridge was also protected during World War II, as were the bridges over Sycamore Creek, Evans Creek, and the Devil's River. However, the troops were headquartered out of Houston rather than locally. As many as 75 to 100 soldiers lived in barracks in a small camp near the bridge. Machine gun nests were placed at each end as well as under the bridge; large guns were placed at strategic points near the bridges.

During the World War II years, the Martin family grew up near the old Central Power & Light Plant on the Devil's River (near the current Air Force Marina). The water near the steam plant, where their father worked, was warm and teeming with fish. Members of the family would catch fish and carry them up to the army camp at the old railroad bridge, where trades could be made. The soldiers liked fresh fish, though their duties did not allow fishing; the Martin children liked the canned goods, candy, and chocolate that were in short supply during the war years. Deals were made, and both sides came away happy.

While little is known about Camp Michie, even less is known about the army camps at the railroad bridges.

8. Neighbors Across the Way

Across the Rio Grande from Del Rio lies the community now known as Ciudad Acuña. In 1870, the governor of Coahuila ordered Captain Manuel Leal to organize a permanent community at that location. It was done that same year, although the founding date of the town is sometimes given as December 27, 1877, under the name "El Capitan Leal," or "Captain Manuel Leal." This second date is used when referring to the town as a new military outpost, so this date may be the formal establishment of the town. In that year the community is credited with 51 families. In 1890, the name of the village was changed to "Villa Garza Galan" to honor a later governor of the state. But by 1894 the name was changed to "Villa de las Vacas," or "Las Vacas" for the small river entering the Rio Grande, the Arroyo Las Vacas.

For the first few decades after the foundings of Del Rio and Las Vacas, Las Vacas remained the smaller of the two towns. In the first decade of the twentieth century, the population of Las Vacas grew to 2,000 or 3,000 residents compared with as many as 10,000 or 12,000 residents for Del Rio. Las Vacas did not have a railroad to bring in population. Immigrants to Las Vacas came overland in wagons from the south.

In 1908, the Mexican Revolution came to Las Vacas. It is possible that some of the population of Del Rio participated in Mexican Revolutionary activities in Las Vacas. What is known is that in the early hours of June 26, 1908, a group of revolutionary *magonistas*, supporters of Ricardo Flores Magón, attacked the army garrison at Las Vacas. Magón had fled Mexico to Laredo in 1904 to establish headquarters for his revolutionary *Partido Liberal Mexicano* (PLM). The engagement proved bloody, lasting several hours. The garrison held, and the attackers fled into the mountains and to safety but with their ammunition exhausted and suffering many casualties. The Mexican government claimed that the attackers had planned their operation in and carried out the assault from Del Rio.

Mexico at the time was governed by Porfirio Diaz, president for most of three decades. His rule was considered dictatorial by many. When the newly assigned Mexican consul arrived in Del Rio, he complained that no Mexicans in his district (Del Rio) had bothered to welcome him or visit him in the days after his arrival.

Las Vacas was settled after Del Rio, but has become a much larger city now known as Ciudad Acuña. (Warren Studio.)

By 1910, official documents stated that most of the Mexicans in Del Rio were "ardent sympathizers" of the revolutionaries.

At the time of the Las Vacas attack, Magón and several other party leaders were in jail in the United States for neutrality violations. These neutrality laws prevented anyone from using American soil to engage in foreign hostilities. Without necessarily admitting any violation of the laws, President Theodore Roosevelt sent troops into the Del Rio area to guard against any other possible violations, and he ordered an investigation.

Luther Ellsworth, the United States consul responsible for the middle Rio Grande communities including Del Rio and Las Vacas, carried out the investigation. Ellsworth wrote that the sympathizers may have helped the attackers. The "common people" of Del Rio allegedly was a base for an "active revolutionary group." The Liberal Party in Del Rio published its own newspaper, *El Liberal*, which, according to Ellsworth, "had influenced and excited to almost madness many . . . and is in a measure responsible for the attack on Los Vacas [*sic*]." Further investigation by Ellsworth, U.S. Attorney Charles A. Boynton, U.S. Marshall Eugene Nolte, and Captain C.H. Conrad Jr., the cavalry commander at Camp Del Rio, concluded that between 40 and 75 men had invaded Mexico from Del Rio using arms obtained in the United States. And in March 1909, several of the liberal leaders were tried and convicted in Del Rio and sent to prison at Leavenworth.

Since its creation in 1924, the United States Border Patrol has been present in Val Verde County. The agency now occupies three separate facilities scattered around town rather than this one, lone building that appears to date to the 1920s. Note the garage in the right background housing more automobiles. Nevertheless, early patrolmen often rode on horseback. (Warren Studio.)

Both the Mexican and American governments were upset about the situation. The Mexican government stationed a consul in Del Rio to keep the central government informed of further developments. The United States government sent special agents to Texas to help detectives find evidence against the *magonistas*. Apparently, further cross-border actions had been planned for 1908 but never enacted. American investigation and law enforcement efforts by the United States Marshals and the State Department were joined by those of the Departments of Justice, War, Treasury (Customs Service), and Commerce and Labor (Immigration Service). Texas Rangers eventually joined the overall effort. Border surveillance consequently increased making further local neutrality violations "too dangerous" near town.

Constant surveillance of the whole border was difficult. The international border in Val Verde County west of Del Rio was the particular subject of Ellsworth's concern. He saw that the rough Texas terrain and brush could conceal crossings by revolutionaries. He noted that the Mexican government did not appear to be making any effort to patrol the area and intercept revolutionists crossing into Mexico. Nearly a year after the attack, during July 1909, the Mexican government finally sent a troop of rurales to patrol the Las Vacas area. On the other hand, the flow of the Rio Grande diminished during a dry fall of 1910, "facilitating the crossing of armed expeditions and the smuggling of weapons." The U.S. government itself, originally, only had three people deployed in Del Rio. American agencies, however, beefed up their personnel deployments.

Nevertheless, Ellsworth concluded on several occasions that the Mexican government had no right to complain until it made a real effort to guard its own side of the border. At a later point in time, he noted that, once again the Mexican government was failing to protect the border and was leaving the United States "to furnish sole protection against smuggling or illegal crossing."

The Mexican Revolution is generally stated to have begun in 1910. Francisco I. Madero was considered the principal threat to the Mexican government, and he eventually became known as the father of the revolution. Madero was riding a wave of pre-existing anti-Díaz feeling that was very strong in the Borderlands because radicals, including Ricardo Flores Magón, had been rising up for years. As November 20, 1910 (the date scheduled for Madero's general uprising) neared, large numbers of "Mexican secret service men" appeared prominently on the American side of the border. American and Mexican troops stepped up patrols. Nevertheless, the Revolution began. No other immediate revolutionist crossings into Mexico were recorded in Val Verde, Ellsworth noted, because the entire neutrality force—cavalry troops, marshals, Secret Service agents, and others—stayed on alert the entire night. However, over time, some of the *magonistas*, like those in Del Rio, did enter Mexico and fought on their own in the Revolution, while others joined Madero's supporters as *maderistas*.

Because the Rio Grande forms the international border, travelers between the two cities have to pass through Customs, although the facilities in 1913 were much more modest than they are now. (Whitehead Memorial Museum.)

75

Following the initial phase of the Mexican Revolution, reports of more cross-border activities continued to occur. The Mexican government sent so many complaints during 1910 and 1911 to the U.S. State Department that the complaints were ignored. Mexico's Ambassador León de la Barra said that, at least on one occasion, revolutionists at Las Vacas crossed into the United States and from American soil fired on Mexican troops. While unproven, the continuing situation concerned Ellsworth. He personally inspected the border by driving from Ciudad Porfirio Diaz (Piedras Negras) to Las Vacas. Once again, he concluded that the American side of the border was sufficiently guarded but that Mexican troops were failing to guard their own side of the Rio Grande.

It seems that complaints about neutrality violations were made because of the Mexican government's failure to understand American law. While agents of the Departments of Justice and Treasury kept munitions dealers in San Antonio and elsewhere under surveillance, they could not arrest dealers for selling weapons. Nevertheless, Mexican government agents also kept the dealers under surveillance and often told them that selling munitions could land the dealers in jail. The U.S. government did try to prevent munitions from being smuggled out of the country, but gun-runners were careful and West Texas was larger than the government's ability to patrol consistently. Stories of revolutionaries and gun-runners in Comstock, Langtry, and towns farther west have been part of the history and lore of the Trans-Pecos.

Del Rio's sister city, known as Villa Acuña during the early 1900s, was and is a popular tourist visit for Americans. Mrs. Crosby started a cafe in Del Rio, but then relocated across the river. (Warren Studio.)

Crosby's dates to the 1930s. The bar served drinks, and the restaurant has been a staple for lunch and dinner for locals and visitors. Mrs. Crosby's picture is inset at right.

The Mexican Revolution also affected Del Rio in a non-violent manner. Fighting on the south side of the Rio Grande often created refugees fleeing the battlefields to the United States. Eagle Pass and San Antonio were the most prominent destinations for families seeking refuge, but Del Rio also served in this capacity. Greenwood Park served as a temporary campsite for refugees, and there Del Rioans often provided food and clothing to them.

No further Val Verde incidents of confrontation seem to have occurred for some time, although some gun-running through Comstock in 1911 was reported and soldiers from Carranza's army and from Pancho Villa's army were recorded to have camped in Mexico across from Langtry in 1913 and at other times. While the northern Coahuila area across from Langtry might not seem a good place to camp, its out-of-the-way location and Langtry's immediate proximity to the international border and the railroad provided a good venue for arms buying and importation. Revolutionary armies could send representatives into Langtry to pick up arms and quickly retreat back into Mexico before American authorities could intercept them.

In 1914, fears of Mexican Revolutionary activities once again spilled over into Del Rio. According to a contemporary newspaper report, a body of *huertistas* estimated between 300 and 1,000 strong had arrived at Las Vacas. Rumor said that an attack on Del Rio was planned. No attack actually occurred, but distant thunder and lightning flashes made it seem as if the Customs House was under attack by artillery. Hailstones pounding on the town's rooftops contributed to the

The first formal crossing point between Del Rio and Ciudad Acuña was this ferry crossing over the Rio Grande. Boats carried people and goods, horses and carriages, and eventually automobiles before a bridge was constructed. (Whitehead Memorial Museum.)

impression. Speculation of the day was that the many agencies guarding the border near Del Rio, including an extra troop of cavalry, were substantial enough to deter any cross-border action. Nevertheless, nerves were occasionally on edge.

Once the fighting was substantially over, many Mexican families returned to Mexico using Del Rio as their last stopover before crossing over. Thirty miles south of Las Vacas/Acuña is the town of San Carlos. The Mexican government was developing (or re-developing) irrigation projects there and selling land at favorable prices to returning families. Hundreds of families, coming in wagons and automobiles, traveled through Del Rio in 1930 to San Carlos and points south.

During the Revolutionary period, the work of a poet named Manuel Acuña became popular. Manuel Acuña was born in Saltillo, Coahuila, on August 27, 1849, and "is best remembered for the fact that, smitten by unrequited love, he dedicated his final poem to his beloved and then committed suicide." His "premature" death occurred on December 6, 1873, after completing his poem "Nocturno: A Rosario."

Venustiano Carranza, one of the more famous revolutionaries and governor of Coahuila, honored the poet by changing the name of the little town to "Villa Manuel Acuña" on February 16, 1912. Over the years the name was shortened by usage to "Villa Acuña," and Carranza would go on to bigger things, becoming president of Mexico in 1914.

In the summer of 1957, the population of Villa Acuña stood at 13,000. With the growth of the town, Mexican authorities announced a change in its name. On September 16, an auspicious day, Villa Acuña became "Ciudad Acuña."

Del Rio and Ciudad Acuña have been linked across the Rio Grande for more than a century. An old ferry seems to have been in operation as early as 1883. During that year Del Rio officially became a port-of-entry with a customs house.

The ferryboat was attached to a cable stretched across the Grande; no rowing or other manual labor was needed because the ferry was set at an angle and the current would push the boat to the far side. Once there, reversing the angle forced the current to push the boat in the opposite direction. Some merchant trade existed between the two towns; wagons drove along Griner and other streets carrying goods to and from Mexico.

This ferry was supplemented by a wooden bridge in 1922. The bridge from Del Rio across to Las Vacas, called the "Citizens Bridge" was "the longest bridge connecting the United States with Mexico" at the time. Most of the distance covered by the bridge was not over the Rio Grande but over the vega, or brush-covered floodplain. In 1929, the Citizens Bridge Company built a covered tollgate and offices. The gate was on Loop Road, one of the more scenic drives (by horse-and-buggy or automobile) in Del Rio. Bridge traffic was cut by the flood of September 1, 1932. The bridge survived but the long ramp across the vega to the bridge was destroyed; it was repaired and back in operation by January 1933. While the old, wooden bridge was sufficient for foot and cart travel, and even automobiles at slow speed, the greater traffic of modern days necessitated a newer, stronger structure. The new bridge, made of steel with a concrete foundation, was also built in 1929 alongside the old wooden structure, which was destroyed by fire

The first bridge over the Rio Grande near Del Rio was a low, rickety wooden construction. The second bridge, shown here, was more substantial, built of concrete and steel.

in 1945. The new bridge was also higher than the old, able to carry traffic during times of high water.

The City of Del Rio bought the bridge land properties and the bridge on August 27, 1954, using the proceeds from a bond issue. In preparation, the city had extended its city limits out to the bridge site during 1953; the October 9 city referendum vote went seven to one in favor. However, the great June flood of 1954, which caused much damage to Ciudad Acuña, washed out the three-quarter mile approach ramp over the vega. The bridge itself survived, but the transfer of operations and ownership to the city was delayed. Before taking title the city required the Citizens Bridge Company to rebuild the ramps to their pre-flood condition. When the title was transferred, the purchase cost to the city was $504,000. Tolls continued to be paid based on the 1928 schedule: 25¢ per car and driver and 10¢ for each passenger. While sturdy, the bridge nevertheless aged and was replaced with a new structure in 1989; that bridge is the one currently in use.

The bridge was built over the river itself. The south entrance to the bridge connects directly to Ciudad Acuña, but the north end is some distance from the north bank of the vega—the low floodplain of the Rio Grande. A wooden ramp connected the bridge to the Del Rio side of the riverbed. The bridge survived fire and flood, though the ramp's occasional destruction forced travelers to walk through the brush of the vega and climb temporary stairs or ladders to the bridge itself. (Warren Studio.)

9. OUTLAW AIR

Del Rio and Acuña were once home to the world's most powerful radio station. The story began with John R. Brinkley in Milford, Kansas. Brinkley became wealthy in the 1920s performing a controversial rejuvenation operation in which he implanted slivers of goat glands into the human body. He advertised on radio saying, "A man is only as old as his glands." He was known by millions as "Goat-Gland" Brinkley, or simply, "the goat-gland man," and he performed so many operations that Kansas is said to have run low on goats. Brinkley had to import goats from Arkansas, and for each of the thousands of operations that he conducted, he charged $750. Goat glands were used because bull glands were "too strenuous," whereas ape glands were "too short-lived and prone to disease." Brinkley used Toggenburg goats because they were "practically diseaseless and their glands strongly resembled those of *Homo sapiens.*" He made enough money with these operations that when his engineers told him it would cost $36,000 to build special tubes for his Acuña station's transmitters, he is reported to have reached into his pocket and handed over 36 $1,000 bills. His income was said to be in the six figures; later during the Depression, it may have been seven.

In order to promote his business, Brinkley began operating a radio station, KFKB, "Kansas First, Kansas Best." This preliminary experience would pay off for Del Rio some years later. He also ran for governor of Kansas three times. The first time he announced, he had to run a write-in campaign. He is supposed to have made a strong showing, but the vote counters threw out ballots with "t's" not crossed and "i's" not dotted. This strict interpretation was legal, and Brinkley lost, placing third. The second place finisher lost by only 251 votes out of 600,000, but neither major party candidate wanted a recount, which would risk a Brinkley win. Brinkley also lost two later elections, in 1932 and 1934.

Brinkley came to Del Rio when his radio license was revoked by the Federal Radio Commission. (Neither his clinic nor his advertising were approved of by government officials.) Banned from operating American radio stations, he won a permit to broadcast from Mexico. His permit allowed him to build a station anywhere along the border from Ciudad Juarez to Matamoros. Early in the search, he considered buying a station in Reynosa. However, the Del Rio Chamber of Commerce found out about Brinkley's desire for a station, contacted him and

John R. Brinkley is arguably Del Rio's most famous resident. His voice was heard on the radio across the country and around the world. (Dr. Brinkley's Doctor Book.)

suggested that he build across the river. The chamber of commerce arguments were many: the climate was pleasant, officials from Villa Acuña were willing to provide 10 acres of land, Del Rio had an airfield for Brinkley's plane (with a big arrow painted on the roof of the Roswell Hotel pointing towards it), and Del Rio officials would help get all of the necessary permits.

Dr. Brinkley was the great-grandfather and founder of border radio. His station was also one of the first commercial broadcasting successes. In June 1931, he sold his Kansas station, built XER in Villa Acuña and began broadcasting with 100,000 watts. (The Mexican border blasters were all designated with call letters "XE.") Most radio stations in the United States at the time broadcasted a mere thousand watts of power each. In autumn of 1932 he won permission to increase power to 500,000 watts, making XER the most powerful radio station on the planet. His broadcasts were reported to be received "quite dependably" in New York City. Anyone between the Rocky Mountains and the Appalachians could pick up the broadcast, and they were very popular. Brinkley later was also given permission to broadcast on a second wavelength.

DR. BRINKLEY'S DOCTOR BOOK

PRESENTED
WITH THE COMPLIMENTS
OF

DR. JOHN R. BRINKLEY

DEL RIO, TEXAS

Dr. and Mrs. Brinkley and Johnnie Boy greet you and wish you health and happiness and the best of everything.

The Brinkley residence in Hudson Gardens residential section, Del Rio, Texas.

Brinkley's whole family participated in XER/XERA radio presentations and advertising. (Dr. Brinkley's Doctor Book.)

Mexican officials were willing to give Brinkley such latitude with the permits because they were generally upset at a 1924 decision by Canada and the United States taking most broadcast wavelengths for themselves: 6 for Canada and 100 for the United States. Consequently, they were happy to allow Brinkley to broadcast in a manner detrimental to American broadcasts. Brinkley did not even have to leave his Kansas clinic; he recorded his broadcasts on records, which were shipped south and broadcast. Mexican officials protected Mexican radio listeners by erecting giant steel towers to block the signal.

In 1933, after his second loss for governor and facing increasing pressure and criticism from the medical establishment, Brinkley closed his Kansas clinic and moved to Del Rio. He bought and enlarged what is now the Brinkley Mansion on Qualia Drive on the south side of town. From his backyard he could soak in the sun and see the towers of XER rising into the sky just a very short distance across the Rio Grande. His broadcast tower was called the "Queen of the Air," his station "The Sunshine Station Between the Nations." And every day Dr. Brinkley invited America to Del Rio "where Summer Spends the Winter."

Del Rio welcomed Brinkley and his family. A new hangar was built at the airfield because Brinkley had his own airplane. And when he first arrived, the City threw a party in his honor. Before Brinkley, the only radio Del Rio had seen was a homemade set of copper coils wound around an oatmeal carton using

Dr. Brinkley came to town and set up his clinic in the Roswell (on the corner of Garfield and Griner), occupying two floors of Del Rio's most modern hotel. The Doctor Book *contains a long narrative of symptoms a person might have that indicated that a serious examination should be conducted by the Brinkley Clinic immediately. (*Dr. Brinkley's Doctor Book.*)*

COSTADO NORTE DE LA RADIO DIFUSORA
NORTH SIDE RADIO STATION
VILLA ACUNA COAH. MEX.

Radio XER was the world's most powerful radio station in its time, a subject of tourist visits and postcards in the United States and Mexico.

an old phonograph horn as a speaker. Its broadcast range was measured in feet; Brinkley's was measured in hundreds and thousands of miles. Brinkley's 300-person payroll ran $20,000 dollars per month, and he was known for donating to many charity causes on both sides of the border. "Del Rio thrived during the depths of the Depression." While "thrive" may have been an overstatement, any town surely would have welcomed an enterprise of that size during the Depression.

Once in Del Rio, Brinkley opened a clinic in the Roswell, occupying several floors of the newly built hotel. Brinkley had abandoned the goat gland operations in Kansas during the summer of 1933 (shortly before arriving in Del Rio) because, he declared, "we have commercial glandular preparations that we can buy on the market and inject to take the place of the glandular transplantation." Brinkley was injecting his patients with "mercurochrome"—which turned out to be water with indigo coloring. He also injected patients with testosterone and sometimes hydrochloric acid diluted in water.

Dr. Brinkley and his radio station were repeatedly in and out of trouble with the governments of Mexico and the United States. During the early days of XER, the Mexican government prohibited Brinkley from crossing the international bridge into the country. Brinkley responded by establishing a special telephone line from XER to a remote studio in the Roswell Hotel from which he broadcast. In response, the United States government banned the practice of telephoning outside the country for rebroadcasting back into it. So Brinkley again used the technology of "electrical transcription"—the recording of the speech and music on aluminum disks. The records were then shipped to the station and played at 33 and 1/3 (but from the inside groove out).

XERF may be remembered for its country music and rock-and-roll, but a great many styles of music were sent out over the airwaves, including gospel. This booklet, available at a modest cost, allowed listeners to read or sing along to the radio. (XERF Specially Selected Hymns.)

Brinkley's station was shut down by Mexican authorities in February 1934 under a newly declared policy of shutting down the border blasters, apparently starting with XER. New regulations prohibited foreign studios from broadcasting in Mexico as well as all non-Spanish medical programming without special permission from the government. Consequently, a radio inspector from Mexico City tried to close XER. Brinkley was so popular, though, that local officials, local soldiers, and Acuña's townspeople threatened to lynch the inspector. But when the inspector returned with non-local troops, the citizens backed down. Brinkley was off the air.

Brinkley was off the air only temporarily. He began broadcasting from XEPN at Piedras Negras and XEAW in Reynosa. Knowing he might lose access to those, he even considered refitting his yacht, the *Doctor Brinkley II,* as a floating station. He was finally able to work out a new permit with the new Mexican government of Lázaro Cárdenas, and on December 1, 1935, Brinkley started his station anew with the call letters XERA. The station broadcast at a rated 500,000 watts, but it also had a third antenna to the south that acted as a directional antenna sending the signal northward at a strength of 1 million watts. Stories of XERA are as outlandish as they are common. Ranchers picked up the signal on their barbed-wire fences. In Acuña electricity sparked on waterheaters, window screens and dangling wires; so much current was in the air that unconnected wires could light up lightbulbs.

During this time Brinkley opened a second clinic, in San Juan, Texas, to treat "problems of the rectum." Brinkley advertised, "Remember, San Juan for rectal troubles, and Del Rio for the old prostate." On occasion, Brinkley continued to use XEPN and XEAW, both nearly as powerful and able to cut farther across American wavelengths. As he said, "Radio waves pay no attention to lines on the map."

Radio XER, XERA, and the others were full of fringe characters who were not generally welcomed by American authorities. (Brinkley's stations also broadcast Spanish-language programming, but those hours and programs were not controversial.) Among them was Dr. Mel-Roy, Ps.D and Ms.D, the "Apostle of Mental Science," whose *Book of Dreams* explained to audiences the secrets of the subconscious world. Sam Morris, the "Radio Temperance Lecturer" told Americans about the evils of alcohol. He explained that alcohol was the true reason why nations fell from positions of prominence and power.

Modern television evangelists can trace their roots to Dr. Brinkley's border blaster. American networks had adopted policies prohibiting radio religion. Even when preachers could buy airtime in the United States, they were prohibited from soliciting donations on the air. So they went across the border, bought their time, and asked for their donations—on XERA and its successor XERF. Reverend George W. Cooper, a former moonshine runner from North Carolina, cowboy evangelist Dallas Turner, and Reverend Frederick Eikenreenkoetter II (Reverend Ike), who called himself unreal and incredible to those with limited consciousness, all made rounds on the Del Rio border blaster. Dr. Gerald Winrod

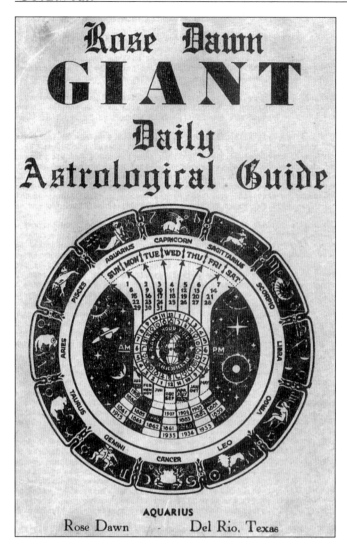

Rose Dawn GIANT Daily Astrological Guide

AQUARIUS

Rose Dawn - Del Rio, Texas

Rose Dawn offered these yearly astrology guides, though she noted, "It is up to you to make the most of what I have given." The text includes material about the character and temperament of the person and makes comments about romance, health, domestic affairs, and business. The booklet also presents a 365–day guide of things to do, or not. (Rose Dawn Giant Daily Astrological Guide.)

pushed cancer cures, scripture, and attacks on communism while Brother Mack Watson and Brother David Epley sold holy oil, prayer cloths, and even "the hem of His garment."

During the Brinkley era, astrology and psychic hotlines were illegal in the United States, so the border stations were home to astrologers and psychics of the day. Among the "quacks" and "spooks" on Brinkley's station was an astrologer named Rose Dawn, the "Star Girl of Radio XERA," who came to Del Rio from Hollywood. There, she had been in show business as a singer, dancer, and showgirl—dancing at some of the hottest night spots. But then she got into astrology.

Rose Dawn's Del Rio operation was as simple as it was profitable. She developed astrological charts, storing them in floor-to-ceiling wall shelves. There was one for each day of the year, but she also took into account place and time of birth. If a person had been born on a ship at sea, the place of birth was to be written in longitude and latitude. She would then chart where the various astronomical bodies were at the time of birth. With this information, she would describe a person's character and main events of the person's life.

When a person sent in a dollar, she sent out one of these strips. The mail truck would arrive at least once per day with five or six bags of mail. "Practically every letter had a dollar bill in it." All of the mail went by Rose Dawn's desk, where one or two longtime entrusted employees opened the letters and took out the dollar bills. They passed the requests and return addresses on to other employees who checked the birth date and place, found the appropriate chart, put the chart in the envelope, and addressed it to the sender. This went on hour after hour, day after day, for more than seven years; several people were kept busy full-time.

Some of the letters were broadcast on Rose Dawn's radio show in the late afternoon. She would read the selected requests and give the astrological predictions. But she also mixed in some Christianity by saying things like "We will pray for you." This statement led to another, like "We will pray for you in our chapel," which led people to believe that Rose Dawn had a chapel. When visitors began coming to Del Rio to visit the chapel, she quickly set aside part of the office building and made one.

Rose Dawn's partner and husband, Koran, is not as well remembered, and his full career has not been recorded. In his early days he was a practitioner of stage magic and was known as "The Novel Conjurer" and "That Conjuring Cuss." Advertisements later called him "The International Forecaster" and "The Mediumistic Sensation of Europe." These last titles give an idea of his stage presentation with crystal balls, spirit seances, and the "actual visible materialization of spirit forms." He also made claims of predicting the future, a talent that coordinated well with the Star Girl's astrological activities.

Rose Dawn was also known as the "Patroness of the Sacred Order of Maya." Del Rio, according to the pair, just happened to be a center of the ancient Mayan culture. In the pursuit of spiritual enlightenment, they bought a dude ranch at Bandera, Texas. There, they revived the secrets of the Mayan order. At the ranch, several stones were erected in such a manner as to resemble Mayan or Aztec structures. There were even altars, though no blood-shedding occurred. Rather, after the short ceremonies, a party atmosphere prevailed. Regular dude ranch activities, such as horse riding, were common as well. But it was spiritual enlightenment that Koran advertised on "Radio Brinkley."

Among their other projects Rose Dawn and Koran published their secrets of success in a book called *The Revelation Secret*. In those sacred pages, readers could learn the secrets of mind and spirit, of fulfilling their wishes, and increasing their incomes—all for the minimal cost of one dollar (to cover the costs of printing and postage). The booklet seems to be a combination of generic Christianity and self-help book. Corinthians and the Gospel of Mark are quoted along with such platitudes as "Do every practical thing, no matter how little, to bring about fulfillment of your desire. . . . It is the formulae of Joan of Arc, of Napoleon, of Kublai Khan, of every self-made person who has accomplished great things" and "Don't reject any good desires because it seems unattainable." The book also includes a short "history" of the Maya and an explanation of their secrets of life. After nearly eight years, the Del Rio operations were shut down. Rose Dawn and Koran moved to San Antonio, where they kept some sort of astrological operation going, but nothing quite like those in Del Rio and Acuña. The Order still operates out of San Antonio as a self-help organization; letters from the Order still bear Rose Dawn's signature even though she died in 1957. Koran had died in 1953.

Incidentally, Rose Dawn and Koran's house still stands on Griner Street at the west end of Canal Street. In that very large backyard, the two threw parties and entertained friends and other people from the West Coast and elsewhere. She drove a large, pink LaSalle automobile, a very prominent and visible display of her wealth. Other brightly-colored Cadillacs were used to drive visitors around town or up to the Bandera ranch.

Brinkley left Del Rio in 1938 with his career already in decline. He moved to Arkansas after several Texas lawsuits and the establishment of a cut-rate competitor, but he commuted back to Del Rio on Thursdays to broadcast on XERA. He opened two hospitals in Little Rock, but judgments resulting from lawsuits began eating into his fortune. In 1939, Brinkley lost a local libel suit against "longtime Nemesis Dr. Mossis Fishbein" one of the people accusing Brinkley of being a quack and of using the hard sell to gain his patients and their money. At the trial, Brinkley wore his hundred-thousand dollar diamonds. Outside the courtroom he sponsored a publicity contest. Contestants were to complete the sentence: "I

This house, built on Griner Street by a man named Patton, who had come to Del Rio to build the Roswell Hotel, is the home in which Rose Dawn and Koran resided.

consider Dr. Brinkley the world's foremost prostate surgeon because ——"; and XERA offered the prize.

Despite the publicity, he still lost. Brinkley appealed but lost again. He also lost court cases in Arkansas, and even the Internal Revenue Service filed a "Texas-sized claim" against him. After "fruitful conversations" between American and Mexican communications officials and the signing of an international convention regulating broadcasts, XERA was "deleted" from the realm of Mexican broadcasting. The American government agreed to clear six frequencies and make them available to Mexico. While in Mexico City to try to renew his permit, Dr. Brinkley received a phone call from his station manager: "Did you know that the Mexican army is tearing down the station right now." On March 29, 1941, radioman Brinkley was off the air—permanently.

In his last days, Dr. Brinkley tried putting several last-ditch plans into effect. He consulted Rose Dawn about his running for the presidency of the United States. The reading was apparently bad, but he did file for U.S. senator from the state of Texas. He also announced that he was going to move his clinic back to Del Rio. It never happened; Brinkley suffered a blood clot in August 1941 and he lost his leg. Convalescing in his San Antonio home, he saw his last on May 26, 1942.

Brinkley's operation and that of Rose Dawn and Koran brought prosperity and glamour to Del Rio during the Great Depression. No streets were named for them; Rose Dawn and Koran are often not even remembered. But those people spent money "wildly." They also provided many local residents with regular employment. With nationwide advertising, people came from all over just to spend their money in Del Rio. Other than the railroad and the military at Fort Clark, Brinkley radio and its related operations were the biggest payrolls between San Antonio and El Paso prior to the Second World War.

During Brinkley's heyday, the Brinkley Mansion was a source of entertainment for Del Rio residents. People would drive out to the house to watch the dancing fountains bought from the Chicago World's Fair and the flashing colored lights while listening to the Brinkleys' pipe organ, played by Joe O'Toole. People could even put in requests, and O'Toole would play them. (O'Toole seems to have been multi-talented: organ player, bodyguard and tutor for the Brinkleys' son.) The organ was inside the house, but loudspeakers were mounted out on the fence. Inside the fences the Brinkleys also maintained a menagerie, including peacocks, large tortoises (which sometimes blocked the drive), and even kangaroos for a time. For the convenience of the community's spectators, Brinkley built a parking lot in the cow pasture across the street from the house.

The mansion was also the origin of Del Rio's Brinkley Lumber Company. When the Brinkleys bought the house, they expanded it to near twice its former size. According to Brinkley's wife, the local lumber merchants gouged Brinkley, and so Brinkley started his own lumberyard to "give them some competition." The business remained active for several years.

Brinkley died in 1942, but his legend, like the echoes of distant signals, lived on. His success had inspired other border blaster stations like XEPN in Piedras

Negras, XEAW and XENT in Reynosa, and XERB near Tijuana. Authors Gene Fowler and Bill Crawford report that in 1934 "nine superpowered stations along the Rio Grande were either operating or authorized to begin construction. The aggregate power of these nine stations was a whopping 2,432,000 watts, an astounding figure, considering that the combined wattage of all U.S. stations at that time was a meager 1,700,000 watts." These stations were popular, at least in part, because they could reach the rural areas of America that urban stations could not.

As for the Acuña station, former Brinkley associates won permits to reopen it under the call letters XERF. Don Howard and Walter Wilson approached Arturo C. Gonzalez, who had dual Mexican and American citizenship as well as the connections to cut through the red tape. Gonzalez had handled legal matters for Brinkley and was "an especially effective negotiator." In 1947, XERF began broadcasting at "fifty thousand watts clear channel." The term "clear channel" referred to the fact that the station was the only one broadcasting on that particular frequency. Without other stations clouding the airwaves, the XERF broadcast had better reception across the entire country, even without the huge XER transmitter, which had been taken to Mexico City for Radio XEX. Still, the lower-power 50,000 watts then carried as far as 250,000 watts in the late 1980s. Radio XERF had "great coverage of the entire USA" at 1570 AM on the dial, but only at night. During the day, "you're burning up a lot of electricity just to get to San Antonio." But at night, the signal went on and on.

Many famous personalities made names for themselves on XERF including radio announcer Paul Kallinger. After World War II, Kallinger came to Del Rio to work for KDLK, a 250-watt station at the time. He then moved to the 5,000-watt KPLC at Lake Charles, Louisiana. Kallinger came back to Del Rio and to XERF in 1948 as a disk jockey and pitchman. As a pitchman, Kallinger sold almost anything: razors and household goods, rose bushes, and lawn and garden items. Kallinger remembered being accused of selling autographed pictures of Jesus Christ, but "We'd never do that on X-E-R-F. I think they did it on X-E-G." The pictures were part of border blaster mythology. Author Tom Miller pursued the legendary pictures, but at every station, broadcasters insisted the ad was on some other station. Miller reported that "Although no one has actually seen one, everybody readily concedes the autographed pictures do exist."

Kallinger broadcasted from ten until two—the graveyard shift—and played country music, which was not called country but "hillbilly" music, with mandolins and banjos. The station also played bluegrass until it "graduated to country music." Kallinger hosted such celebrities as Eddie Arnold, the Carter family, Porter Waggoner, Tex Ritter, Ernest Tubb, and Johnny Cash. The music was complemented with on-air preachers. Kallinger himself broadcasted out of XERF for 40 years using the station break:

> From coast to coast, border to border, wherever you are, whatever you
> might be doing, when you think of real fine entertainment think of

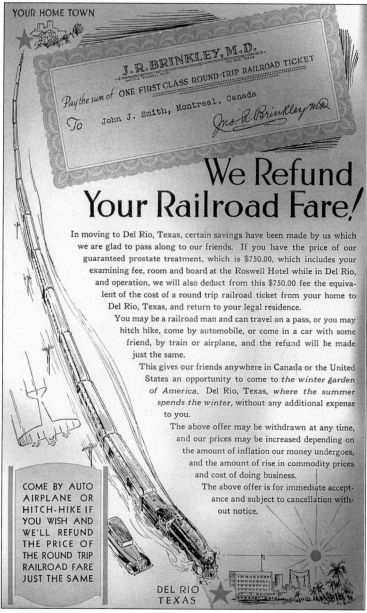

A common theme about the Great Depression has emerged: it was not as bad in Del Rio as it is reported (in history books) to have been on the East Coast and metropolitan areas. Val Verde County had farms and ranches, and Del Rio had Dr. Brinkley bringing a huge amount of money to the city by way of a railroad bringing his patients here to boost the economy. People came to Del Rio by the train-load, each paying $25 (plus lodging and food) to as much as $750 (with everything on the house). (Dr. Brinkley's Doctor Book.)

Paul Kallinger was the voice of Del Rio for millions of radio listeners. (Warren Studio.)

XERF in Ciudad Acuña, Coahuila, Mexico, alongside the beautiful, silvery Rio Grande River where the sunshine spends the winter. This is Paul Kallinger, your good neighbor along the way, from Del Rio, Texas.

Even with the smaller wattage, Radio XERF had the same kind of broadcasting range as Brinkley's XERA. Kallinger once asked listeners to call in to the station to find out who was listening, and from where. Calls came in from 45 of the 48 American states. Kallinger also received calls from Canada, Greenland, England, Germany, South America, Japan, and Australia. It was said that the Soviet Union's KGB even listened in to learn English.

"The King" once tried to get on XERF but was rejected. Kallinger remembered the following:

Elvis Presley's ballads had a little bit of country flavor at the time; he was just easing into the rock field. If he had come up with "You ain't nothing but a hound dog" right from the very beginning, people may not have accepted that transition because it was too fast. In 1955 Elvis called my house in Del Rio after he had just converted to rock and roll. He said that he had just heard Johnny

Cash on my show and that he would like to be on the next night.
I said, "We don't allow rock-and-roll artists on our program." He
said, "Thank you anyway, Mr. Kallinger."

Kallinger later did play Elvis Presley on the radio, but the show was on a
Louisiana station where Kallinger was appearing as a guest disk jockey. Kallinger
was relieved that the King had no ill feelings, but he was adamant about keeping
his show country. Singer Webb Pierce stated "If it hadn't been for border radio, I
don't know if country music would have survived." Kallinger has been even more
blunt: "Country music would not have survived without the border stations."

Another radio announcer named Bob Smith also worked out of XERF. He came
to Del Rio/Acuña from Louisiana thinking there was big money on the border.
He bought control of the station in the late 1950s, altered the programming to
include rhythm-and-blues and rock-and-roll, and changed his on-air name to
Wolfman Jack.

The Wolfman was "the master of shuck and jive." He howled and growled on
the air, barked and chattered, and told his teenage listeners to get naked, kiss their
teachers, and wiggle their toes. He also told them to vote for him for president.
Like Kallinger, he also advertised a variety of mail-order products with his music; "I
tried selling something called Florex which we advertised as a sex pill. The Federal
Trade Commission made me stop. They got a sample and discovered we were
selling sugar pills." It seems that the echoes of Dr. Brinkley had not yet died.

The station under the Wolfman still maintained good relations with the
townspeople of Acuña. XERF had sleeping and eating facilities for its 30
employees, who grew their own food and raised their own sheep and goats. Twice
each month, the station threw a shindig complete with food and music, sometimes
country and sometimes *mariachi*. The cops, *federales*, came on horseback, and
everyone would get "totally blitzed," even while the hellfire-and-brimstone
preachers were on the air.

Another incident told and retold by the Wolfman involves a gunfight for
control of the station. (Kallinger has said that this story isn't true but that "it
makes a good story.") The Wolfman was at home in Del Rio's Roswell Hotel
listening to the station when someone on the air yelled "*¡Pistoleros! ¡Pistoleros!*"
The Wolfman arrived at the station to see "a rival faction . . . like Indians circling
the fort." They were shooting at station people, and station people were shooting
back. Wolfman Jack reported that two of the invaders were killed but none of his
people. Generally though, the station kept in good relations with the townsfolk as
well as the law by paying bribes—"If we didn't come up with the green, nothing
would get done." He even paid to make sure no one went to jail and to have
the whole thing "forgotten about." He spread the green, and "Bob Smith, a.k.a.
Wolfman Jack, became a pirate king. Station XERF was his kingdom." However,
it has been written that "the Wolfman's version often varied with the telling."

An April 18, 1963 labor dispute also affected Kallinger. "Kallinger's departure
from XERF was memorable." An intruder poked him with a pistol while Kallinger

was pitching a commercial at the station; the gunman then walked Kallinger outside and ordered him in Spanish to "run." Kallinger walked, slowly—until he was out of sight of the station. Then he ran. Kallinger said the incident marked his last live broadcast on XERF.

XERF was still growing and building its international reputation. According to the Wolfman, the station "had the most powerful signal in North America. Birds dropped dead when they flew too close to the tower. A car driving from New York to L.A. would never lose the station. I had listeners in New Zealand! I made funny remarks about Khrushchev and they jammed X-E-R-F in Moscow!" The Wolfman turned XERF into his "national institution of radio naughtiness." He had grown up listening to the border blaster, and then made a career on the other side of the mike.

In 1986, XERF went to a Spanish format after the Mexican government had taken over. Station XERF still broadcasts from the countryside west of Acuña in its all-Spanish format; nevertheless, the glory days are over.

Other sad news from the frontier of radio include the deaths of the two most famous XERF broadcasters. The Wolfman died in 1995 after a career that eventually included Hollywood. Paul Kallinger has also passed on, last year in 2001. A lifelong resident of Del Rio, Kallinger is buried in Westlawn Cemetery.

Brinkley and Kallinger both promoted Del Rio and Ciudad Acuña.

10. BLUE SKIES

In 1911, Calbraith Perry Rodgers brought the wonders of air flight to Del Rio while making the first transcontinental air transit in his aircraft called the *Vin Fiz*. The feat started after newspaper mogul William Randolph Hearst offered $50,000 to the first person to fly across the country in 30 days. Rodgers, "a tall, wiry, cigar-chomping, motorcycle-racing daredevil," launched himself on the quest from Sheepshead Bay, Long Island, New York, on September 17, 1911. His aircraft was a Wright Brothers EX model. To earn money during the cross-country transit, Rodgers named the plane "Vin Fiz" after a new grape-flavored soft drink being marketed by the Armour Company of Chicago. The $5 per mile Rodgers received helped pay for costs during the flight.

The aircraft was quite frail, not much more than a motorized kite. The engine weighed 196 pounds, and the whole plane less than 800. The wings were made of spruce covered with "rubberized duck fabric." The plane needed to land often for refueling (and repairs), and Del Rio was one of the refueling points. A special train traveled across the country with a supply of parts, first aid materials, provisions, mechanics, Rodgers's wife, several representatives of the Armour Company, and as rumor had it, a coffin. The three-car train was painted white, and the name of the plane was on each car.

At the time, no airports or air traffic control existed, so Rodgers followed the navigation aids that were on the ground—railroad tracks. "In fact, a 25 mile stretch of tracks of Jersey City, New Jersey, was whitewashed to help guide him." Rodgers passed the 30–day mark while in Oklahoma and, therefore, was disqualified from winning the big prize. The aviator, nevertheless, continued on to Texas and the Pacific.

Each stop was a major publicity event. People loved to see Rodgers performing aerial acrobatics. On the other hand, "Rodgers left a trail of complaints in Oklahoma and Texas as a result of unscheduled landings. His favorite landings were in cotton fields."

In Del Rio, the arrival was such a sight that the school let out so that the children could join the many adults who had gathered to see Rodgers and his plane. He came in late. For two hours, every buzzard in the sky was the plane until, finally, the *Vin Fiz* came into sight. Townspeople staked a sheet on the ground near

Cal Rodgers was a hero in his time, but his untimely death allowed other aviators to set records of faster, higher, and greater duration of flight. (Warren Studio.)

Highway 277 south of San Felipe Creek. Rodgers "was supposed to circle the town before he landed but he didn't." He did not stay long either. Having loaded his pocket with cigars and his aircraft with fuel, he took to the skies, and "all the horses had a fit." He did not stop at Langtry because, at that point, his flight was good, and he wanted to make up time after his crash at Spofford. The flight across Val Verde County went so well that he outraced his train and bought fuel locally at Dryden before flying on to Sanderson.

Rodgers landed in Pasadena, California, his original goal, on November 5 after flying 4,321 miles. Rodgers, however, decided to fly on to the Pacific Ocean. He flew on to the coast at Long Beach, California, and rolled the wheels into the surf. "He had completed the first transcontinental flight after more than seventy stops, numerous accidents, an in-flight run-in with an eagle, and replacing enough parts to build four new aircraft."

During the years of the Mexican Revolution, aircraft were stationed in and travelling through Del Rio on reconnaissance duty for the United States Army. This activity was reported as early as 1915. The airfield was located east of U.S. Highway 277 and south of the railroad tracks. While there was a landing strip, apparently there were no hangars. The pilots would ask local landowners for permission to tie their planes to fenceposts to protect the planes from wind damage. After Pancho Villa attacked Ciudad Juarez in 1919, airplanes from San Antonio and Houston were ordered to the El Paso–Fort Bliss area. Del Rio was one of the stops on the way as the planes flew west to form the Aerial Border Patrol.

Military observation of the border was organized on July 1, 1919, with the creation of an Army surveillance group at Kelly Field near San Antonio. In August, the group was renamed the First Surveillance Group and relocated to Fort Bliss, only to be returned to Kelly in 1921, all the while patrolling the border. One wing of planes was stationed at Eagle Pass, and the pilots often flew over Del Rio on surveillance flights. Occasionally, the planes and pilots were also stationed in town.

Among the pilots stationed in Del Rio was Lieutenant Jimmy Doolittle. Doolittle was a World War I ace, and in World War II would lead the first bombing raid on Tokyo. He spent much of his early career in several Texas posts and was stationed at Eagle Pass and Del Rio from 1919 to 1921, sometimes under jurisdiction of Camp Michie's 12th Cavalry.

While in Del Rio he flew his airplane under the Pecos High Bridge. Doolittle told the story in his autobiography:

> Fifty miles west of Del Rio on the Pecos River near Comstock, there was a Southern Pacific Railroad bridge known as the Pecos River High Bridge. . . . It looked easy to fly under, so I did. But I had to bank the wings nearly vertical to get between the upright piers.

This is an oft-repeated story, but, according to Doolittle, it gets better.

Note the crowd in the background behind the airplane. As small as the aircraft was, it was the first to visit Del Rio (and dozens of other towns across the country); therefore, the Vin Fiz's *arrival was an event. (Warren Studio.)*

A few weeks later, I had a forced landing at Langtry. As I stood around waiting for someone to arrive to help me repair the engine, the biggest, toughest Texan I have ever seen rode up on horseback and said, "I'm looking for the SOB who flew under the Pecos High Bridge and tore down the telephone wires which were strung under it. I'm the lineman who had to swim the river and restring them."

Sensing that he could be in a load of trouble, Doolittle:

expressed sympathy at his inconvenience and advised that I would endeavor to get his complaint to the proper party when I returned to my base. Luckily, I was flying a plane other than the one I had been using. . . . Consequently, the cuts dug in the struts by the telephone wires were not there to indicate my culpability.

Doolittle escaped the wrath of the lineman, but the flying feat is reported to have become a rite of passage for later pilots.

On July 2, 1942, the United States Army opened Laughlin Army Air Field east of Del Rio because the Army "was in desperate need for more pilots very quickly." Laughlin Field was commanded by Lieutenant Colonel E.W. Suarez until December 26, when Colonel George W. Mundy assumed command. Originally

The early history of the B-26 proved less than illustrious. The aircraft acquired nicknames, such as Widow Maker, because of its tendency to crash. The names Flying Prostitute and Baltimore Whore resulted from a common opinion that the plane, with its small wings, had no visible means of support. Later, the wingspan was increased by six feet to stabilize the plane, but its reputation had been made. (Credit AAFTFS, MB., Del Rio, Texas.)

selected as a bombardier school, the post was changed to a training school for B-26 pilots. On February 2, 1943, Laughlin was designated the Army Air Force Transition Flying School, Medium Bombardment, and later, the Army Air Forces Pilot School.

Del Rio native Frank E. Torres was one of the first military personnel at the base. The first people assigned were the engineers and construction crews. Torres:

> was the only Air Force guy there; all the rest were engineers. Col. Suarez was an engineer, and he was in charge of constructing the damn base for the army engineers. And of course, he had his crew there, all his crew, you know, sergeants and corporals and privates and what not. But they all belonged to the engineers for the army, the army engineers, in other words. I was the only aircraft guy there, the only one who belonged to the air force.

When the base became operational, Torres remained, and his bilingual ability was quickly put to use. "About a week or so later, I was put into a . . . squadron. And a plane cracked up in Mexico." Mexico was one of the Allied nations during War World II. Torres continued with the following:

> So they needed somebody that spoke Spanish to go with the crew to bring the body and the wreckage back and everything. So, I said "I know Spanish." They said, "You're it." So I went with the crew just as an interpreter. There was a captain, and I think there were about ten guys who went over there in a truck to pick up all the pieces, pick up the body and whatever was there. . . . After that, they had a lot of crashes here because in the old days, you know, they didn't have radar. They flew with what they called dead reckoning, you know. They flew by compass. And at night, they used to fly over here and go crash . . . in the Sierra Madre Mountains in Mexico. They had about . . . twenty five over there; and every time they had a crash, they needed somebody to speak Spanish to go up there with the crew to bring up whatever what was left. So I stayed there for three and a half years as an interpreter and taking care of the colonel's airplane. And all my army career was here in my own home town.

As the air base was being deactivated after the war, Torres "had the distinction of being the last serviceman to remain on the base. He flew aboard the last plane leaving the base before it became completely closed."

Laughlin Field itself was named for Lieutenant Jack Thomas Laughlin of Del Rio. Lieutenant Laughlin was the first pilot from Del Rio to be killed during the Second World War. Lieutenant Laughlin had been flying over Java on January 29, 1942, in a B-17 when he was killed. Special dedicatory ceremonies were held on March 28, 1943, with Lieutenant Laughlin's family in attendance.

The naming of the Field for Lieutenant Laughlin required a certain amount of effort on the part of the citizens and boosters of Del Rio. While Del Rio residents may take for granted the name of Laughlin for the Air Force Base, Army policy of the early 1940s prohibited the naming of military installations after individuals. A telegram sent May 16, 1942, from J. Autrey Walker, chairman of the Val Verde County War Savings Committee and vice president of the Del Rio National Bank to the War Department, promoted the idea:

> SINCE DELRIO [sic] IS NOW ASSURED US AIR TRAINING SCHOOL I WOULD AGAIN LIKE TO SUGGEST THAT THE FIELD BE NAMED IN HONOR OF LT JACK T LAUGHLIN U S AIR CORPS KILLED IN ACTION IN THE FAR EAST ON JANUARY 29 LT LAUGHLIN WAS FIRST DELRIO MAN TO LOSE HIS LIFE IN THIS WAR.

This telegram was not well received. Army memos detailed a plan of action to reject all such requests. A line in one of the internal memos did leave the door open: "It seems to me we should obtain more information in regard to Lieut. Laughlin to find our whether or not the field at Del Rio later could possibly be named after him."

Exactly what threw the door open to the naming might have come from Congress. Representative Charles L. South of the 21st District (including Southwest Texas) began promoting the idea and sending letters to Army officials. His requests were initially rejected, but he and others persisted. Exactly when and how the name change was effected by the Army is unknown. Nevertheless, the field was named for Lieutenant Laughlin.

Life in Del Rio during World War II was in many ways similar to that in towns across the country. "Big Brother" kinds of government regulation were commonplace. Shoes were rationed; the law allowed a person to buy only three pair per year. The selling of shoes was prohibited entirely on certain days. The same applied to canned food; sales were prohibited for a time while a rationing program was put into place. People were limited in the number of cans of food they were allowed to buy, and at the beginning of the program, each family had to report to the government how many cans of food the family had in its household. To buy food, one had to have permission from the government in the form of ration coupons, and the newspapers were full of notes telling the public when the coupons could be used and when not. And this was in addition to the daily appeals that each person spend at least ten percent of his/her income on war bonds.

Other government regulations had particular impact on rural communities and counties like Del Rio and Val Verde. Automobile tires had to be inspected every four months to make certain they were not "abused," and tires had to be registered with the government to make certain that no one was hoarding. This was a particular hardship because of the prickly and thorny brush on the county's ranches. Furthermore, ranchers were allowed to buy ammunition only

The original appearance of this image was on the front cover of The Twenty-Thirtian, *a magazine catering to pilots. Jack Laughlin is on the left; friend and fellow pilot Johnny Atkinson is with him. Both had received their appointments as second lieutenants in the Officers' Reserve Air Corps and were also featured in "Flying Cadets," an article in that same issue. The photograph is a phony, a fabrication. The two pilots are not standing in front of the aircraft in the background. Nevertheless, the photo has been commonly reproduced locally. This copy appeared in the June 30, 1967 issue of Laughlin Air Force Base's* Border Eagle, *the base newspaper. (Laughlin Air Force Base, United States Air Force.)*

The original photo was doctored, but here it has been doctored further. Lieutenant Atkinson has been severed from the image. This appeared in the Border Eagle *of July 2, 1982. (Laughlin Air Force Base, United States Air Force.)*

once every three months even though inadequate rounds meant predators would kill livestock.

One issue that had to be addressed by the government was that Del Rio did not have sufficient housing for the increasing numbers of residents due to the base's creation. At one point, base commander Colonel Mundy complained that Del Rio residents were not doing enough to support the war effort. Nevertheless, residents donated services such as library books and dance partners for the young G.I.s. For this, Colonel Mundy commended Del Rioans "for their contributions to the war effort."

Laughlin Field remained active during the war, but closed shortly afterward. During the war, the base was considered temporary. Water wells had been dug, but they brought up sulfur water, which was not drinkable; therefore, water was trucked in from Del Rio. No water main linked the field to Del Rio's water supply as there is now. In August 1945, the deactivated field and facilities were turned over to the Army Corps of Engineers, and some of the land was leased to local ranchers.

Unlike many other communities, the end of World War II did not severely impact the economy of Val Verde County. Del Rio had no real war industries, and few industries existed exclusively on Army business.

Laughlin and the war ended, but Laughlin did not die. In 1947, the United States Air Force was created by dividing the Army Air Forces from its traditional ground units. The new U.S. Air Force became very important, and eventually the Air Force returned to Del Rio.

In May 1952, Laughlin Field was reopened as Laughlin Air Force Base. This is significant because many former wartime military posts were never reactivated. Garner Field in nearby Uvalde, once closed, closed permanently.

As important as the reactivation was, a 1954 announcement of "Permanent Installation" was just as important. In September Senator Lyndon Johnson and Representative O.C. Fisher telegrammed Del Rio officials that "Laughlin will take its place as a part of the permanent Air Force Base structure." This designation had been sought for a long time by the Del Rio Chamber of Commerce because it meant that several building programs on base, such as family housing, could be continued or accelerated.

Laughlin Air Force Base is a sizable institution. The Base is 3,961 acres large, but its allocated airspace is 9,200 square miles. This airspace was especially useful when, in October 1952, the Air Force decided to use the base for jet training. Laughlin's reach had become global by the time of the Cuban Missile Crisis of 1962.

The 4080th Strategic Reconnaissance Wing was moved to Laughlin on April 1, 1957. The first six planes arrived on June 11. Unarmed but equipped with incredible cameras, the now-famous spyplanes were called the ultimate Cold War aircraft. The U-2 was a project originated by the Central Intelligence Agency (CIA), approved by President Eisenhower, and administered jointly by the CIA and the Air Force. On July 29, 1955, Tony LeVier conducted the first taxi test and, inadvertently, the first test flight. (The aircraft lifted off the runway at a slower speed than expected.) The first official test flight happened on August 4 of the same year.

Operation Crowflight, the U-2 mission at Laughlin, included sampling the air at high altitudes for radioactive materials. The Defense Atomic Support Agency was investigating the effects of nuclear detonations because they were concerned with the increasing amounts of uranium, plutonium, and other radioactive isotopes in the air. By figuring out how much material was in the high atmosphere, the agency might be able to figure out how much could come down. For the next seven years, beginning in October 1957, the U-2s flew thousands of miles at altitudes between 50,000 and 70,000 feet, channeling air through special filters to collect the particles. The U-2s were also used by the CIA for intelligence gathering.

While the U-2s and their missions were generally kept secret, one of the pilots exposed the craft within days of their arrival in Del Rio. All of the people associated with the aircraft were under strict instructions to keep quiet; the men were not even allowed to tell their wives. However, on June 28, less than three weeks after their arrival, Lieutenant Ford Lowcock flew over Del Rio at a very low altitude, over his house on Avenue P, where he lived with his wife and two children. During one of his turns, his U-2 struck a hill near the airport and crashed. Lowcock was killed. That same day, north of Abilene, another Laughlin U-2 crashed, killing pilot Lieutenant Leo Smith. Other U-2 flights claimed several casualties quickly, but there was also one spectacular escape. On September 26, 1957, pilot and squadron boss Jack Nole, who had brought a flight of U-2s to Laughlin, bailed out of his aircraft from an altitude of 50,000 feet. He survived, setting a record for the highest altitude parachute jump at that time.

As a general rule, however, most people in Del Rio did not know about the missions of the U-2s until 1960. Missions were often flown at night, and aircraft maintenance was done in secret. In 1960, Laughlin AFB acknowledged the presence of U-2s as evidenced by a press release printed on May 5 after the shoot-down of a U-2 over the Soviet Union. Colonel A.J. Bratton, the 4080th commander, stated that none of the Laughlin U-2s were missing.

The U-2s were publicly displayed for the first time on November 2, 1960, at Patrick Air Force Base in Florida. Earlier, on October 24, President Eisenhower had visited LAFB, where he saw the planes and visited with the pilots while in Del Rio to sign documents starting the building of Amistad Dam. It was his first direct observation of the U-2. Francis Gary Powers had been shot down during Operation Overflight over the Soviet Union earlier in the year, forcing Eisenhower to admit to the existence of the plane and its mission. The U-2s were finally made public at Laughlin on May 14, 1961.

The 4080th Strategic Reconnaissance Wing at Laughlin played an important role in the Cuban Missile Crisis. On October 14, 1962, Major Richard S. Heyser flew over Cuba. The film images showed missile sites. The next morning, Major Rudolph Anderson Jr. shot photos of similar sites, giving the U.S. government conclusive evidence of the introduction of Soviet long-range missiles into Cuba.

This was a find—the proof of the faked photo. This comes from a poor xerographic copy of Mary Laughlin's scrapbook full of photos of her husband during his pilot training in California and Utah. The original shows Jack and friend in a hangar looking at some aircraft outside the frame of the image. The editors of The Twenty-Thirtian *superimposed a copy of that print on top of a picture of the background aircraft in an effort to better illustrate the magazine cover. (Val Verde County Historical Commission.)*

Laughlin Air Force Base was home to the super-secret U-2 spyplanes during the 1950s and 1960s, including the time of the Cuban Missile Crisis. Security at the base, therefore, was important.

Numerous other U-2 flights were ordered and carried out. On October 24, Soviet freighters were stopped en route to Cuba. The crisis was resolved with the Soviets' removal of offensive missiles from Cuba and the United States' removal of offensive missiles in Turkey. Only one American was killed by enemy action during the crisis: Laughlin's Major Rudolph Anderson. During the morning of October 27, Anderson was flying a route over Cuba away from known surface-to-air missile sites; nevertheless, a missile downed the plane and killed him.

The U-2s completed their mission at Laughlin on July 12, 1963, when the 4080th left for Davis-Mothan Air Force Base near Tucson, Arizona. At 10:30 a.m., Major Patrick J. Halloran flew the last Laughlin U-2 off the runway, circled the town of Del Rio, and disappeared into the western sky. During the wing's time at Laughlin, the men were decorated with numerous awards, including a posthumous award of the Distinguished Service Medal to Major Anderson.

Even before the Strategic Air Command left Laughlin, the base had been turned over to the Air Training Command. The 3645th Pilot Training Wing was activated in October 1961, and the first training aircraft arrived November 1. The handover of jurisdiction occurred April 1, 1962; the first class graduated December 7. With young pilots once again in the air testing their flying skills, it was not surprising that some tried to repeat the feat of Jimmy Doolittle. Unfortunately, a couple of them did not make it. On April 18, two pilots, instructor First Lieutenant J.E. Lingan and student Second Lieutenant L.W. Ellefson, died in a T-37 jet trainer when it hit telephone lines stretched across the Pecos Canyon 500 yards south of the Pecos Highway Bridge. Other crashes have occurred, mostly on or near the runway. Among them were those of November 1969, April 1974, and December 1996. In each of these crashes, the pilots fortunately survived.

Jet training continues to take place at Laughlin. The 47th Flying Training Wing was activated on September 1, 1972. The Air Training Command has three squadrons of trainers operating on base. The T-37 Tweet is used for general pilot training by the 85th Flying Training Squadron. The 86th Flying Training Squadron uses the T-1A Jayhawk to prepare pilots for tanker aircraft, while fighter pilots are trained on the T-38 Talon of the 87th Flying Training Squadron. These squadrons along with the 47th Operations Support Squadron collectively form the first of three base organizations: Operations Group. The others are the Support and Medical Groups. Each is designated as "47th" and, collectively, compose the 47th Flying Training Wing. Interestingly, Laughlin is commanded by a colonel rather than a general. However, Laughlin is smaller and limited in its operations. Nevertheless, when Laughlin commander colonels are transferred away, they tend to be promoted to general in a way that suggests that the base is a training ground for generals as well as pilots.

Laughlin Air Force Base has established a historical display of nine planes at the aptly named Heritage Air Park. The park is located inside the main gate to Laughlin AFB, but after the terrorist attacks of September 11, 2001, access to the park will likely remain limited.

On the west side of Liberty Drive are four of the aircraft. The first is an F-84F, a more modern version of the 60 F-84Ds that were used at Laughlin from 1952 until 1954, when they were transferred. The second is a T-33 training aircraft used to observe unmanned drone targets, for radar intercept training, and for calibrating radar site equipment. In June 1953, 40 of these planes were at Laughlin; the planes remained in use over Del Rio through 1964. The AT-6 Texan World War II trainer is still flying in foreign countries. Used at the beginning of the Second World War elsewhere, these aircraft first arrived at Laughlin in 1944 and were used at the base through 1945. Lieutenant Jack Laughlin flew in this type of aircraft during his training. The fourth and final aircraft on the west side of the park is another training aircraft, the T-28A.

On the east side of Liberty Drive sit five other displays. The fifth, farthest from the gate, is a Douglas A-26B Invader. The accompanying plaque states that this plane was "dedicated to those of the Army Air Force Transition Flying School at Laughlin Field who flew and maintained" this aircraft. The fourth plane is the EB-57B (B-57). This aircraft was the first foreign-designed aircraft used by the U.S. military after the Second World War. Different models of this aircraft were flown at Laughlin from 1957 until being replaced by the U-2s. The middle plane in this row is the Lockheed U-2C of the 4080 Strategic Reconnaissance Wing. The plaque in front of the display U-2 at Laughlin contains a quote dated November 26, 1962, from President John. F. Kennedy: "The work of this unit has contributed as much to the security of the United States as any unit in our history, and any group of men in our history." The second plane is a small trainer, the T-34, and the display nearest the main gate is a UC-45J, which was used as a staff transport and light personnel transport. The "J" indicates that this version had special features, such as an improved exhaust system and a more aerodynamically shaped, extended nose. Three of these aircraft were at Laughlin Field by October 1944 and were stationed here through the end of the war. Versions of this aircraft were also used at Laughlin Air Force Base after its reopening through 1958.

The dedication of the U-2 Blackbird display was special. Held on May 24, 1987, over 200 members of the 4080th/100SRW Reunion Association joined retired general and former Wing Commander Austin J. Russell to dedicate the U-2C, serial number 66707. "Their thoughts turned to Anderson, of course, but also to many others."

A more recent commemoration was held at Laughlin on October 26, 2001. Wing Commander Colonel Rick Rosborg wondered aloud, "I can't tell you why it's taken 39 years to honor Major Anderson." The occasion was the renaming of the base's Operations Training Complex to Anderson Hall. Major Anderson's wife died in the 1980s, but two of his three children, son Jim Anderson and daughter Robyn Anderson Lorys, attended the ceremony. A plaque "In memory of Major Rudolf Anderson, Jr." was dedicated with the knowledge that all future Laughlin pilots, teachers, and students would pass though the doors of Anderson Hall.

Heritage Air Park is found immediately inside Laughlin Air Force Base's main gate. (Laughlin Air Force Base History Office.)

11. THE LAND OF AMISTAD

The area around Del Rio is prone to flash flooding. The soil is thin; the ground is rocky. West Texas is normally dry, but when the thunderstorms come, the rain they drop fills the draws and arroyos quickly. The Devil's, the Pecos, and the Rio Grande have all been repeatedly inundated by flashfloods. Del Rio generally does not suffer the ill effects of flashfloods because the city is not built on a riverbank as are Ciudad Acuña, Eagle Pass, and Laredo. For example, the floods of 1930 and 1932 did not greatly impact the city of Del Rio; although the Flood of 1932 destroyed the great pecan trees of the Devil's River canyon. Roads and highways were often closed after flashfloods washed out sections of road. Del Rio might be cut off for a couple days, but the city itself would be okay. In 1935, the circumstances changed.

The worst flood in Del Rio tore through the town on the night of June 13, 1935. The early part of summer brought strange weather to West Texas. The entire state had been suffering from a drought in 1933 and 1934, and Val Verde County had been suffering as well. March 1935 brought one of the worst storms in Del Rio history. The storm of March 21 brought 56 mile per hour winds, a record for the community, and 2.5 inches of rain between 7:15 p.m. and 8:30 p.m. The city also saw a "brilliant electrical display" and a great deal of damage all across the city. Streets were flooded; as much as 3 feet of water flowed down North Main Street. Fences, roofs, and garages were blown away. Many trees were knocked over. San Felipe Creek rose 10 feet, and flagstones at Roosevelt Park were washed away. The most costly damage was at the tank farm where 25 empty crude oil tanks sat east of town. They had been built at a cost of $25,000 to $40,000 each. Twenty-one of them "crumpled."

Rains in April, May, and early June dumped large amounts of water very quickly in localized areas. One town might get 2 inches in a couple hours, but nearby towns would see nothing. May 1935 set records for rainfall with 13 storms during the month and 4.89 inches of rain, 2.01 inches above normal. June 5 saw two-thirds of an inch, but on June 11, 2.18 inches fell. This last rain fell over a wide area, closing highways north and south out of town and raising San Felipe Creek and the Rio Grande 6 feet above normal. Two more inches fell on Del Rio during the day on June 13 raising the Rio Grande to 12 feet above normal. The

Del Rio once had a petroleum refinery (east of town), which included this tank farm. Most of the tanks were destroyed during a storm in 1935. (Val Verde County Historical Commission.)

Devil's River was flowing over the power plant dams, highways west, north, and south from town were closed, and the railroad was closed because of a washout of track near McKees west of town.

That evening, the sun set. When it rose again, Del Rio was in shock. Some of the newspaper reports were graphic: "The screams of the drowning could be heard for blocks above the roar of the creek." By daybreak of June 14, four were known to have died, and a dozen were missing. Over 50 homes were demolished or swept away, and more than 200 people were homeless.

All of the local creeks and rivers overflowed their banks. The Rio Grande had risen to cover the vega, and the San Felipe Creek had risen into the San Felipe neighborhood. Volunteers had canvassed the low-lying areas with warnings to evacuate, but many did not heed them. North of town, the Devil's River canyon was swept by a 35-foot wall of water. The water flowed over the tops of the power plant dams, and the facilities had been abandoned during the night. Water submerged the power plants upstream, rising 4 feet over the tops of the buildings, but did not get into the steam plant near the mouth of the river. The flow in the Sycamore washed out the approaches to the bridge and cut off highway access from the east, and the highways north and south were closed as well. The railroad was cut off by floodwaters west of town. The railroad bridge over the Sycamore held, but the railroad bridge over the Nueces was destroyed when it was hit by a house carried by the floodwaters.

Rainfall amounts for Thursday night, June 13th, were impressive and threatening: half an inch fell between 10:25 and 10:30 p.m.; 6 inches fell between 7:00 and 11:00 a.m.; and 8.88 inches fell between 7:00 a.m. Thursday and 7:00

a.m. Friday. The 24-hour total was a record, but that rain had fallen on top of several earlier hard rains and swollen rivers. The June total, up to the 14th, was 13.70 inches. This was half an inch more than all the rain in 1934, and twice as much as the 1933 total of 6.79 inches.

With totals such as these, the damage was extensive, and the stories from the 1935 flood were terrifying. The newspaper reported this gut-wrenching account (which has the same feel as accounts after Del Rio's 1998 flood):

> An unidentified woman slipped from the clutches of Tomas Cuellar and Francisco Lomas, members of a rescuing party. The men, standing in water five feet deep, had grasped the woman by the wrist when a large wave collapsed the porch on which they stood. The woman's screams as she was swept away could be heard for several minutes above the angry roar of the waters.

Her body was found several days later almost completely buried in mud and gravel. Only her hand protruded from the ground. The rescuers felt great apprehension as they moved into a South San Felipe neighborhood called the Devil's Corner, or Rincon de Diablo. It was thought that the warnings might not have made it to that area.

Even with the warnings, the severity of the damage could not be escaped. Water flowed through Brown Plaza knee-deep; cars were swept away; household items floated in the water; more debris was hanging high in the trees. Twelve-foot square pieces of pavement were picked up and knocked aside. All of the bridges across the Creek were under water. The approach to the U.S. Highway 90 bridge (over the east creek) was eroded, but the bridges survived. The 200-foot-long bridge on the Eagle Pass Road was knocked out, along with the gas pipeline anchored under it. In the neighborhood the floodwaters submerged all of the bridges—on Johnson/Taini Street, at the Old Pig Pen Crossing at Moore Park and on Academy—and all of the approaches were badly damaged. The new Canal Street Bridge (which was still under construction at the time) survived, and work on it was rushed to get the bridge into use. When the waters receded, the bridges at Johnson/Taini and Losoya/Gillis were revealed to have been destroyed. Academy was repaired by Friday, but San Felipe Creek did not fully recede back into its banks until Saturday.

Other bridges around town and nearby also suffered. The bridge on Loop Road (needed to get to the International Bridge) was destroyed, as was the bridge on the road to Lake Walk on the Devil's River. Road damage in town was so bad that estimates said six months would be required to fix it all.

At the time of the flood, the city had been preparing to place new pumps in the springs for the city water system. The foundation for the new pumphouse had been poured, but no other work done. The floodwaters had reached the top of the 8-foot protective walls around the springs and then rose another 10 feet above the top. "Had our pumps been there, they would have been ruined," commented one city engineer. Taking the flood into consideration, the city decided to place the pumps into the creek bed, but into a waterproof, underground vault.

The Red Cross was the principal relief agency after the flood. San Felipe School No. 1 was used as an emergency shelter for some 200 people. The call went out for cash, food, clothing, kitchen and household items, shoes, and bedding. The local chapter raised $500, received a $500 match plus another $250 later from the national organization. "This [$1,250] will be sufficient to meet minimum needs," said Gertrude Girardeau of the National Disaster Reserves. One hundred twelve families received relief from this fund, with most families getting $5 or $6.

Fortunately for the town, the common post-flood problems, such as disease, did not occur. Mosquitoes proved to be those of the nuisance variety rather than the kinds that transmit malaria. Nevertheless, the city poured oil on pools of standing water in an effort to minimize the problem. Four cases of typhoid were reported shortly after the flood, but just a few days later, the city health officer stated in no uncertain terms that only one case was known and that it was not a result of the flood. He stated that the Del Rio water supply was clean and disease-free. However, it was reported that San Felipe was being served by a single 2.5-inch water main. Gardening and clothes washing were prohibited in San Felipe until a larger replacement pipe could be laid.

In all, the Flood of 1935 was the worst disaster the city of Del Rio had ever experienced—until 1998.

The Central Power & Light steam plant near the mouth of the Devil's River was subjected to flooding because it was situated within the river's canyon. Herbert Martin and others had to work through the flood and clean the facilities of mud and muck after the 1954 flood, shown here. The men went to work in a boat. (Dudley Martin and Daisy Speer.)

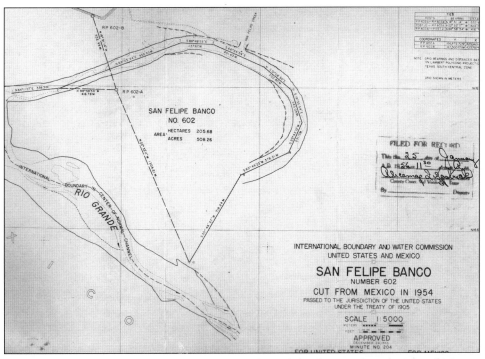

The floodwaters from June 1954 carved a new channel for the Rio Grande. Part of Mexico then ended up on the American side of the river. In 1955, the International Boundary and Water Commission declared the territory, called a banco, to be part of the United States, therefore making the United States a few acres larger. (Val Verde County Clerk's Office.)

Floodwaters once again rose in local streambeds in June 1948. The storm that brought this flashflood struck more locally. The Rio Grande rose a few feet, but floodwaters in Devil's River severely damaged the steam plant. The damage was not as bad as that of the 1932 flood when nine workmen were trapped on the roof of the plant. The fact that the plant survived demonstrates how solidly built it was. Del Rio remained intact; the floodwaters raced around the city into the Rio Grande.

The Flood of June 1954 did less damage to Del Rio. However, it caused extensive damage across the Rio Grande in Ciudad Acuña and downriver. The flood actually began far away from the Rio Grande in Ozona, Texas, in Crockett County. Eighteen inches fell on Ozona in 21 hours with the runoff flowing down the Devil's River. Five people were drowned in Ozona; one of the bodies was found only 12 miles north of Del Rio. One car was washed 5 miles downstream and buried; the male occupant was found dead floating in the water; the female occupant was not found and presumed drowned. Farther west, unofficial reports at various ranches gave higher rainfall numbers, and much of that runoff went into the Pecos or directly into the Grande. The Pecos, the Devil's, and the Rio Grande all flooded with 20 to 35 inches of rain on the rivers' watersheds.

Many parts of Del Rio were under varying amounts of water during the Flood of 1954. Since so much of the San Felipe neighborhood lies within the curves of San Felipe Creek, high water, shown here, washed through Brown Plaza and nearby areas. The floodwater did not, however, top the Canal Street Bridge, at left. (Warren Studio.)

Floodwaters were so high in the Devil's River canyon that 2.5 feet of mud was left on the second floor of the steam plant near the mouth of the river.

This flood followed what appears to be the standard pattern for Southwest Texas. Rainfall for 1954 had been below normal, then in mid-June a thunderstorm broke dropping 1 to 2 inches over town and up to 5 inches on some parts of the range. The swollen Rio Grande closed the International Bridge for a day and crested at over 21 feet. A group of illegal aliens was washed away as they tried to enter the United States across the river; seven were found dead during the following days.

The flood to come was heralded only as "light to moderate rain." An inch of rain fell in town, but north and west the torrents fell, and from June 26 to 29, news of destruction filled the papers. Highways were closed; bridges were washed out, and the low-lying areas of Acuña were submerged. Over 10,000 people had to be evacuated to higher ground. As the water began falling, damage assessments began. "Not 20 percent of the homes [were] left in the low areas." The U.S. Fourth Army from San Antonio was feeding 10,000 Acuña residents a day, with the Red Cross paying for the food itself. The charity work ended half a year later after the United States had given 2 million pounds to Acuña. Noted, particularly, was one

Captain Joseph L. Bowler, assigned to Fort Sam Houston and flying during the relief effort. The local newspaper called him the "hero of Korea, who is credited with a world's record of 482 helicopter combat missions in ten months to bring out the wounded. During three days he set another unofficial helicopter record flying to Ciudad Acuña a total of 740,150 pounds of food supplies, averaging 2,471 pounds an hour, setting down for 190 landings."

The railroaders were stopped in their tracks. Washouts east and west of Langtry stranded the Sunset Limited, and 13 Air Force helicopters were brought in to airlift the passengers and crew to Comstock. Bonney Vineyard described the effects of the 1954 flood from a railroader's point-of-view:

> the last one was, we were out here at Devil's River in the siding one night and—oh, it was raining, it was pouring. And I went, put on all the rain gear I could find and went to the telephone, and I asked the dispatcher where this train was we were supposed to meet. And she said "Oh, he's in trouble, behind some high water at Langtry." And I said "Well, you'd better get me out of this Devil's River canyon or I'm going to be in trouble with some high water." He got us up to Comstock [and then] went off duty. I stayed there four days; tracks were washed out ahead of us and behind us. . . . [T]he Devil's River was washed out, and there was some big fills at Langtry, there were some dirt fills over there that were thirty feet high, they built those fills across the, across a little canyon, they'd put in a big culvert. There was a big culvert, and the rain was such that the culvert wouldn't handle the flow from the canyon, and it started running over track. Well, when it did, those dirt fills went right quick. The weather bureau said they didn't know, they didn't know how much it rained, but there is reliable evidence that it rained between twenty and thirty inches up on the Pecos above Langtry.

The stranded trains were serviced by helicopters. Food was flown out to the trains since washouts fore and aft blocked them completely, and the 260 passengers were ferried out on the return trip. The choppers, along with private and Civil Air Patrol airplanes, also flew food and water across to Acuña and were flying search-and-rescue missions along the Devil's River and near Juno and Langtry.

Much of the 12 miles of railroad track between Del Rio and Devil's River was washed away, and railroad service did not resume for nearly a month. Out of 250 miles of road in Val Verde County, 56 of them were washed out. Also washed out was the low-water crossing at the Pecos between Langtry and Pandale. The road north of Comstock was out, cutting off Juno from the rest of the county.

The International Bridge was shut down when one of the ramps was destroyed. Crossings resumed on July 7, when the water had gone down and a ladder was raised so that foot traffic could cross. People had to walk three-quarters of a mile across the vega to get to the bridge itself. A wooden ramp allowing the resumption of automobile traffic was completed August 6.

All of this happened with less than 3 inches of rainfall in Del Rio itself. The four-day total, June 26–29, was only 2.54 inches. June's rain total for Del Rio was only 4.34 inches. Consequently, most of Del Rio survived the flood intact. (Interestingly, a storm that October was described as "the most violent thunderstorm in years" even though much less damage resulted. Six inches of rain fell on Nicholson in South Del Rio, while 4.81 inches fell at the International Bridge. The same amounts of rain were believed to have fallen across the river.)

In the border towns, flood damage was extensive. The crest of the Rio Grande at Del Rio beat the previous record from September 4, 1932. At Del Rio and downriver, the crest surged over 50 feet and as much as 60 feet. It was called "the Rio Grande's greatest flood in history." Del Rio and Acuña, Eagle Pass and Piedras Negras, and Laredo and Nuevo Laredo all suffered from the high waters. As the Rio Grande retreated to its banks, Piedras Negras unofficially suffered over 60 dead and 400 missing. The town of Laredo was divided by the floodwaters, which backed into some creeks and blocked roads cutting off the old town and business district from Laredo Air Force Base and the rest of town. The international bridges and international railroad bridge were all submerged. The border was declared a federal disaster area.

Nevertheless, an aerial survey watched the muddy floodwaters wash into the Falcon Reservoir—where the waters stopped. Falcon had only begun impounding water on August 25, 1953. The floodwater almost filled Falcon Reservoir bringing the water level to 295.9 feet above sea level—within half a foot of the conservation level of 296.4 feet. (Conservation level is the height of the water behind the dam that is planned to be stored.) The flood provided enough water for the power plant to begin production. More importantly, Falcon stopped the rush of water, and no flooding occurred downstream in the valley.

Falcon Dam's proven flood control prompted the United States and Mexico to plan a second major dam upstream. Even before the cleanup was over, Del Rioans were suggesting an accelerated timetable for construction. Senator Lyndon Johnson promised to begin the work on funding for the project. The International Boundary and Water Commission visited Del Rio and investigated potential damsites nearby. The site chosen lay a short distance up from Del Rio at the confluence of the Devil's River with the Rio Grande.

An October 4, 1954 announcement about the dam location was welcomed heartily by the Del Rio community. Statistics of bigger and better were rattled off as dollar signs appeared in the eyes of the chamber of commerce. Diablo Dam would be higher than Falcon—280 feet versus Falcon's 130. Diablo would be longer than Falcon by 3 miles. Five thousand new residents were expected to join the Del Rio community; Acuña's population was projected to triple. Del Rio was going to be a "Mecca" for travelers and tourists.

Preliminary reports highlighted the great need for the Diablo Dam for flood control and for agricultural use downstream. Approval of the project was made contingent upon a promise that it "must not impair or diminish the amount of water allocated to lawful diverters and appropriators below Falcon Dam," the farmers using irrigation in the Lower Rio Grande Valley. The governor of the State of Texas, Price Daniel, heartily approved of the project, but because of the international nature of the river, federal government approval was needed. President Eisenhower supported the project and personally "prodded Congress for action" on the project. In the Congress, Senators Lyndon Johnson and Ralph Yarborough pushed the project, and in the summer of 1960, construction of the dam was authorized. The only hurdle was a Senate amendment that stated that any electrical power–generating station in the dam would have to operate on a "self liquidating basis." It would have to pay for itself, and the facility would not be installed during the original construction. No particular dollar amount was authorized for the construction; instead, all appropriations would be made as needed in "such sums as may be necessary."

The massive dam project was renamed "Amistad," the Spanish word for friendship. The original project name was "Diablo Dam," after the nearby Devil's River. Presidents Eisenhower and Lopez Mateos are credited with the change of name. During a preliminary meeting at Camp David during October 1959, President Eisenhower commented that "Diablo" was an "ominous" name, so President Lopez Mateos offered "Amistad" as more representative of the two nations' cooperation on the project.

The meeting of presidents was surrounded by great crowds of well-wishers and celebrants. Here the presidents of Mexico and the United States wave to the crowd from the balcony of Ciudad Acuña's municipal palace (city hall). (Warren Studio.)

119

The rivers near Del Rio contained many fish, including large fish such as this 72.5 pound yellowcat caught near the steam plant. The creation of the larger Amistad Reservoir resulted in much more surface area for fishing. Rumors state that some of these giant catfish are still in the river basin, and six foot long alligator gars are commonly caught. (Dudley Martin and Daisy Speer.)

On October 24, 1960, President Dwight Eisenhower of the United States and President Adolfo López Mateos of Mexico met in Ciudad Acuña and agreed to the project. The arrival of President Mateos was especially celebrated in Acuña because he arrived by special presidential train—the first train to arrive in the city on the newly completed railroad line, heralding the opening of railroad service to and from the city. President Eisenhower flew into Laughlin Air Force Base and motorcaded through Del Rio to Ciudad Acuña. Ike was welcomed by huge crowds of Del Rioans before crossing the international bridge into Acuña, where he was welcomed by the Mexican president and more crowds. From the balcony of the Municipal Palace (city hall), the two presidents welcomed the gathering. This crowd is significant in light of the fact that the day was chilly and a light drizzle was falling. President Eisenhower nevertheless "rode in an open car, bareheaded, waving graciously and flashing the grin which is well known."

The modern celebration of Fiesta de Amistad has its origins in this October 1960 meeting. The Fiesta de Amistad was created to commemorate this meeting, and the celebration has grown annually. Fiesta de Amistad now includes an Arts and Crafts Fair, the Miss Del Rio Pageant, the Grand International Parade, the International Bike Race, musical concerts, and a jalapeno-eating contest. The main event is the Abrazo de la Amistad, the embrace of friendship, which is held on the Amistad Dam between the mayors of Del Rio and Ciudad Acuña under the two great eagles that top the dam.

Amistad Dam was created primarily for flood control—to control floods like those of 1954 and another during 1958, which both killed people and caused serious property damage along the Middle Rio Grande. The dam site is 1 mile below the confluence of the Devil's River with the Rio Grande, which puts the dam in the best position to control floodwaters from the Devil's and the Pecos, the sources of the highest floodwaters along the Rio Grande. Other benefits include water conservation for agricultural irrigation downstream, electrical power generation, and water recreation. Recreation was not mentioned in the earliest authorizations but seems to have become part of the plan in 1963. Great parks could be built because the highways that led directly to and across the reservoir would bring tourists from across the state and from across the southwestern United States and northern Mexico.

Once the construction project was approved by Congress, the many details began to be worked out. Bids were let, timetables drawn up, and related projects begun. In July 1960, President Eisenhower had signed the Amistad legislation, appropriating the first $5 million. This was used to pay for the preliminary surveying and for land purchases at and immediately around the dam site between 11 and 12 miles upstream from Del Rio. Negotiations were underway in early January 1961 for the government to buy the necessary land. Central Power and Light representatives suggested that the company could relocate their soon-to-be

In this 1974 photograph, all 16 gates of Amistad Dam are open. (Warren Studio.)

inundated steam plant; however, that plan proved unfeasible. Both the upper and lower dams would become valueless once Amistad began holding water.

Both the highway bridge and railway bridge would prove inadequate. Both had been built and rebuilt to carry traffic high over the water of the Devil's River, but the reservoir's level would swamp even them. Construction on the new bridges began shortly after the dam was approved. Preliminary plans stated that the bridges would have to be almost as high as a football field is long and cost approximately $5 million. The dam project itself was originally expected to cost almost $70 million, but once work began, expectations increased that figure to about $80 million: $52 million for the construction itself and $28 million to buy the land and rights-of-way. Mexican officials gave their approval as President Eisenhower and the Congress had, and in negotiations, a formula for cost and payments was derived. Because the United States was going to receive more benefits than Mexico, the United States paid for a higher percentage of the project: 56.2 percent versus Mexico's 43.8 percent.

Many of the "details" of the Amistad project were huge in their own right. Eleven and a half miles of U.S. Highway 90 had to be relocated, and a new 5,460-foot bridge needed to be built so that it was high enough and long enough to carry traffic over the reservoir. The highway bridge is longer than the railroad bridge because millions of tons of rock were used as fill at each end shortening the railroad bridge's actual span. The Devil's River Highway Bridge became the second highest bridge in Texas. (The Pecos High Bridge is still the highest.) The

Amistad Dam is topped with the statues of two eagles, the national symbols of Mexico and the United States. (Warren Studio.)

The gates of the dam were all opened to drain high water behind the dam in 1974. This photo suggests that boaters at the time would have had to be very careful crossing under the bridges until the lake could be restored to conservation level. (Warren Studio.)

bridge and the new section of track were opened in April 1963, and the new stretch of U.S. 90 was completed in June 1965. Once completed, the Devil's River Bridge was considered by some to be "the most beautiful bridge in the Southwest." In fact, the structure won one of the American Institute of Steel Construction's 1965 "Prize Bridge" awards. The judges called it "one of the most graceful bridges" they had seen.

While the highway bridge cost about $4 million, the whole of the U.S. 90 relocation cost about $12 million. Some special effort had to be made because several caverns were found to be under the crossing. The caverns were not as large as the caves near Sonora but of the same nature. When they were found, they were quickly explored and then sealed with concrete.

The low bridges on U.S. Highway 277, where the road crossed San Pedro flats, were given up and replaced by a much longer and higher bridge a short distance to the west, at a cost of $1 million. Altogether, 2.7 miles of U.S. 277 had to be relocated. Concrete piers for the U.S. 90 and Southern Pacific bridges rose over 220 feet from the riverbed, but were also anchored downward into the rock 60 feet. The piers are 40 feet in diameter. The Amistad waters were planned to back up into the Pecos River, raising the water level at the highway bridge 60 feet. Even with the extra 60, the water depth at the bridge was 100 feet, meaning that no additional work was needed because of the extraordinary height of the Pecos Bridge. Nor was there any need to work on the Southern Pacific High Bridge farther upstream.

President Johnson and President Diaz Ordaz, on the right, met in 1966 to check the progress of Amistad's construction. (Warren Studio.)

Amistad Dam is a 6-mile earthwork: 4 miles in the United States and 2 in Mexico. The center part of the structure, made of concrete, required 1.7 million cubic yards of material. Tens of millions of tons of rock and earth were laid on either side to hold in the waters once the channel was closed.

The reservoir covers a great deal of land. On the American side of the border, 56,570 acres were needed for the dam and for the water at its highest level. The dam and water covered 37,000 acres in Mexico. That translates into some 135 to 140 square miles of lake. The normal expected water level is 1,117 feet above sea level, which creates a 67,000-acre lake, the third largest international manmade lake in the world. At that level, the lake floods up the Devil's River for 25 miles, up the Rio Grande for 73 miles, and up the Pecos 14 miles. The maximum water height is 1,144.3 feet above sea level which, if reached, extends the lake even farther up each river. For that possibility, the area owned by the National Park Service is larger than the area generally covered by water. This easement is necessary since the primary purpose of the dam is flood control.

The years 1965 and 1966 brought great activities to Val Verde County and Del Rio. Ground-breaking on the Amistad Dam occurred August 1965. And then, announcements were made that President Lyndon Baines Johnson and President Gustavo Diaz Ordaz were coming to meet and see the project. This was their third meeting. Earlier, on November 12, 1964, president-elect Diaz Ordaz had visited the LBJ Ranch, and in May 1965, LBJ had visited Mexico City. For this third meeting, the two presidents greeted one another on the International Bridge on December 3, 1966, proceeded to the Municipal Palace of Ciudad Acuña to greet the crowds of cheering spectators, and flew by helicopter to the dam site to inspect the work. Diaz Ordaz did not visit Del Rio on this occasion or his later meeting with President Nixon because Mexican law prohibited Mexican presidents from leaving Mexican soil. The Mexican president was not even allowed to walk the full length of the dam. (When he visited LBJ's ranch earlier, he was not yet president.)

The dam was completed in 1968. On May 31, Amistad began impounding water behind the dam. The project cost approximately $78 million. While the reservoir did not completely fill until 1972, once a substantial amount of water was behind the dam, more news was announced from the White House.

President Richard M. Nixon and President Diaz Ordaz met on September 8, 1969, to dedicate Amistad Dam. A 300-foot red carpet was brought in from San Antonio—there were none that size in Del Rio—with half on each side of the international boundary across the top of the dam. The speeches were rather short: Nixon spoke for 3 minutes and Diaz Ordaz for 19. Following their speeches, they pulled two cords unveiling a bronze plaque placed exactly on the international boundary. Considering that the Del Rio community and chamber of commerce began lobbying for a dam in this area as early as May 1953, the presidential meeting and dedication must have been most gratifying.

President Diaz Ordaz returned to Amistad and met with President Nixon in 1969 to dedicate the Amistad project and officially open the dam and reservoir for business. (Warren Studio.)

Amistad's water level in 1974 rose so high that some of the lakeside parks were flooded. Perhaps Tlaloc had something to do with it. Tlaloc is an ancient Aztec rain god, and a 40-foot statue of him was constructed in 1969 in a park on the Mexican side of Lake Amistad. (Warren Studio.)

Amistad Dam is topped by two massive bronze eagles. Both Mexico and the United States use eagles as their national symbols. The eagles on the dam during the presidential visit were not the actual bronzes but plaster mockups. Once the ceremony was over, the plaster eagles were taken to El Paso, where the permanent bronzes were cast. William Kolliker of El Paso designed the monuments, and his drawings were sculpted by Manuel Alcala Covarrubias and cast into bronze by Vladimir Alvarado, both of Ciudad Juarez.

The eagles are rich in symbolism. Throughout history, eagle symbols have been used to denote strength and valor. In ancient times, eagles were associated with sun gods and were messengers of the gods. In many civilizations, from Egypt and Rome to Constantinople and Persia, eagles represented kings.

The story of the Mexican eagle goes back to the days of the Aztecs. A long time ago, a people left their land of Aztlan, the Place of Whiteness, led by their god Huitzilopochtli, the Hummingbird of the South, who promised them a new home. The god had promised that the place for their homeland would be identified by a particular symbol or sign. After trials, tribulations, and much traveling, the people arrived at an island surrounded by Lake Texcoco in the Valley of Mexico, and there, they saw the sign. Perched on a prickly pear cactus stood an eagle. Hummingbird of the South said, "O Mexicans, it shall be there!" The year is regarded by the modern calendar to be 1325. In the eagle's clutches was a snake, and on that spot the people built their city, and from that city, the Azteca built their empire.

The American eagle is as symbolic to the American nation as the Mexican eagle is to the Mexican. The symbolism is somewhat different, however, because the

American eagle is not tied to a single, specified event. The American bald eagle is not bald; the name comes from old English and Welsh "balde" meaning "white" and referring to the patch of bright white feathers topping the heads of these birds-of-prey. The bald eagle's commanding appearance and power prompted the American forefathers to associate it with the United States. The wingspan is as great as 8 feet, and when diving, the bald eagle can reach speeds up to 200 miles per hour. The bald eagle is North America's largest bird-of-prey except for the California Condor (which would not have been known to the Founding Fathers at that time). Furthermore, the bald eagle only exists in nature on the North American continent. In 1782, the eagle was placed on the American currency and seal. Any $1 bill will show the bald eagle clutching in one claw 13 arrows, the 13 states united in war, and in the other, an olive sprig with 13 leaves, the 13 states united in peace.

Like the Devil's River bridge over the new reservoir, the dam itself won an engineering prize. The United States Corps of Engineers awarded the Amistad construction with the Engineering Design Award of Merit, for the dam's outstanding design, construction, appearance, and environmental harmony.

High waters returned to Del Rio in 1998. Tropical Storm Charley drifted from the Gulf Coast across southern Texas and then "parked" on top of Del Rio. Amistad Dam captured some of the rain, but more than 18 inches fell on top of Del Rio and the San Felipe Creek watershed, which drains through the city. Some areas north of town saw 20 to 25 inches. Hundreds of people were forced from their homes. Hundreds more risked their lives and safety rescuing them in the middle of the night of August 22–23. Officially, nine Del Rioans died and six were listed as missing.

The Amistad Dam and Eagles have become such a large part of Del Rio's identity that they have been stylized into the logo for the City of Del Rio, shown here on the new Bedell Street water tanks.

127

12. SCHOOLS APART AND SCHOOLS TOGETHER

It is difficult to imagine a Texas school bus without those magic letters—ISD. Before the creation of independent school districts, Texas operated common school districts under county supervision. The creation of an ISD meant an elected school board would oversee the district and levy taxes for the maintenance of the schools independently of city and county government.

It was the summer of 1890 when the voters decided to take action on the education of their children.

> Whereas an application was filed with me as County Judge of Val Verde County Texas, on the 19th day of June, 1890, signed by the requisite number of qualified voters, asking that an election be held within the boundaries hereinafter set forth for the purpose of submitting to a vote of the people the question of incorporating the territory embraced in said boundaries for free school purposes only.

The last part was important. No other county governmental regulation was involved, and the "incorporation" was not a municipal incorporation. Because of this, the school district turns out to be older than the city government.

The election was held July 1, and the vote was overwhelmingly positive. Sixty-five chose "Corporation;" only 16 voted "No Corporation." As a result, taxes were levied on land and animals: sheep at $1.25 per head, goats at 60¢, cattle at $6, and "cow ponies" at $22.

By 1896, tax levies were broadened: goats were up to 75¢, cattle down to $3, grazing land at $1 per acre, and pasture at $1.15 per acre. By 1904, goats were up to $1.25 while "sheering goats" were at $2. Steers were valued at $12, and cows a whopping $50. "Saddle horses" were valued at $20, and "work horses," $30. Watered pasture was valued at $1.50 per acre.

The Del Rio ISD boundaries did not include the San Felipe neighborhood. The declaration of boundaries described the line as starting north of town on San Felipe Creek, down the Creek to the Rio Grande, upriver along the Rio Grande

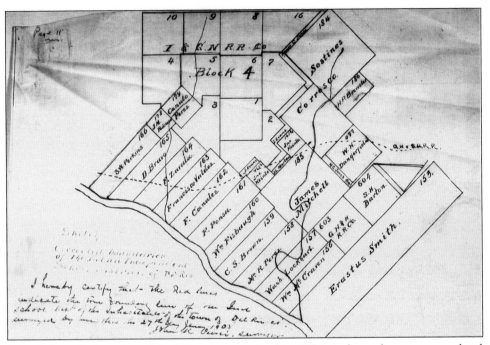

The Del Rio Independent School District, organized in 1890, is shown here on a map dated 1908. (Val Verde County Clerk's Office.)

to the mouth of Cienegas Creek, up the Creek to a point north of the railroad tracks, and back to the place of beginning.

The San Felipe neighborhood is sometimes considered separate from Del Rio (and early city documents generally refer to the area as "East Del Rio"). Having been excluded from the school district, the Hispanic community developed its own schools, collectively called Common School District #2.

The exclusion of the predominantly Mexican-American neighborhood of San Felipe had the effect of excluding most of the town's Hispanic schoolchildren from the better-funded primary schools and from secondary school entirely. However, this also fostered a community spirit, and the San Felipe schools became the heart of San Felipe's identity.

During the 1920s, the San Felipe district operated two schools: San Felipe School #1 and San Felipe School #2. Number 1 had been an old wooden shack until 1908, when it was replaced with an improved structure. A second story was added later. The school was later known as Central School, then the Yellow School, or Escuela Amarilla. Number 2 was a two-room structure built in 1909, though two rooms had been added later.

About 500 students attended, most in first or second grade; the seventh grade was the highest level of instruction. For higher grade instruction, students attended Del Rio Independent School District (DRISD), though their numbers were few.

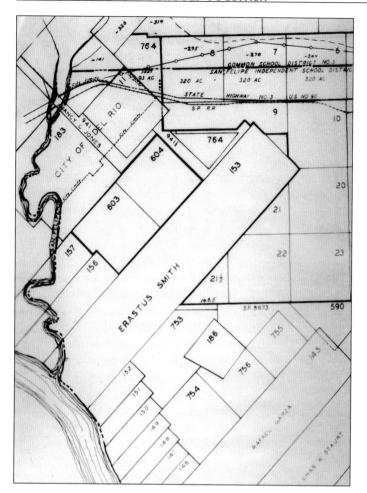

The San Felipe neighborhood had been excluded from DRISD, so the residents created their own—the San Felipe Independent School District—in 1929. (Val Verde County Clerk's Office.)

In 1928, Del Rio I.S.D. annexed a large part of San Felipe/Common School District #2, including all of the San Felipe part of town and both schoolhouses. The officials of DRISD applied to the county school board on June 16 to approve the annexation at the next meeting, June 29. The board did allow people—in favor and in opposition—from the community to speak at that meeting, but, as it is sometimes said, "the fix was in," and the annexation was adopted. Del Rio I.S.D. grew by 23.5 square miles, leaving only the less populated and less valuable property in the southeast corner of the county to District #2.

The leaders of the opposition to annexation included Santos Garza, Hernan Cadena, and Andres Cortina, names now famous in San Felipe community history. The three men were trustees in charge of Common School District #2 and were very vocal in their opposition. Following the annexation, Santos Garza approached attorney Walter Jones of the firm Jones and Lyle and put up $500 cash and a $500 promissory note for a retainer. (Later, community fund-raisers and donations raised $750, which was given back to Garza.)

The opposition leaders went to court and on July 20 won a temporary injunction from the district court, blocking the annexation. DRISD responded August 14 with a motion to dissolve the injunction, and on September 6, Judge Joseph Jones heard presentations from both sides. That same day, Judge Jones ruled in favor of San Felipe and reversed the annexation. DRISD announced its intent to appeal, which was taken to the Fourth Court of Appeals on November 7, 1928. San Felipe won their appeal as well. Issues of race or ethnicity were not part of this court case, as they were in future Del Rio school cases. Nor was there any discussion of personal rights or equality.

For the most part, the case was decided on technical legal grounds. The annexation, Judge Jones decided, would deprive the common school district of its duly chosen trustees and would interfere with the district's contracts with its employees. It would also remove a large portion of the taxable property from the district without its consent, impoverishing the district. Interestingly, the DRISD was $80,000 in debt at the time, which meant that the San Felipe taxpayers would have to pay part of Del Rio's debt (once annexation was completed). The immediate injunction was needed to prevent DRISD from collecting taxes from the area. More importantly, the judge concluded that the annexation of the area:

> was made without the consent or desire of the legally qualified property tax paying voters residing in such contiguous territory sought to be annexed, and without the County Judge of such County having been petitioned by twenty or a majority of such voters.

Therefore, the annexation was done with "utter and arbitrary disregard of the terms and provisions of Chapter 84 of the General Laws of the State of Texas." The annexation further would have increased the size of DRISD to a size larger than allowed under Article 2765 of the Revised Statutes of Texas.

Following the victory, Santos Garza and Rudolfo Gutierrez began discussing the creation of an independent school district for San Felipe. Garza presented a petition to the county school trustees with 200 signatures, which constituted a majority of the "qualified property tax paying voters residing in Common School District #2." The trustees accepted the petition, and a motion was approved July 27, 1929, creating the San Felipe Independent School District. The trustees also ordered an election be held August 31 to choose the seven board members who would oversee the new I.S.D.

August 31, 1929 is the official date for the creation of the San Felipe I.S.D. On that date votes were canvassed and made official. The seven new trustees were Santos Garza, Andres Cortinas, Rudolfo H. Gutierrez, Castulo Gutierrez, Adolfo Maldonado, Victor Vasquez Jr., and Pablo G. Flores. Lots were drawn. The first three men won two year terms, while the remainder won one year apiece. Garza was elected president of the board and R.H. Gutierrez was elected secretary.

One of the first items of business was the creation of a high school, something the new district lacked entirely. Bonds worth $50,000 were issued after a bond vote carried 125 to 0. Ad valorem taxes were established as well (at 35¢ per hundred dollar valuation). On December 13, 1930, the new high school building was opened, completing what is said to have been the only I.S.D. created by a Hispanic-Texan community for a Hispanic Texan community.

During this time of segregation in public schools, Del Rio played an important part in the integration and civil rights movements. In the early part of the twentieth century, the Del Rio Independent School District established its position firmly on the side of segregation, but later adopted integration easily and without the violence that so often accompanied this issue.

Hispanics in Texas found themselves in unusual legal and social circumstances. In the early part of the twentieth century, Mexican-Americans were counted as "white" in the United States Census. Only in 1930 was a separate category created for Hispanics: "Spanish surnamed." And the (1876) Constitution of Texas, while authorizing separate schools for blacks and whites, did not authorize the segregation of Hispanic students from other white students. Nevertheless, Hispanics generally were segregated. In 1955, the United States Supreme Court ruled that all laws, federal or state, that required segregation "must yield

When Common School District #2 was limited to offering lower grades only, the San Felipe Independent School District extended its offerings to include high school. The Old San Felipe High, shown here, is now used as a middle school in the San Felipe Del Rio Consolidated Independent School District.

The identification of this building is uncertain, but it seems to meet the description of the "Mexican School" in the 1930 civil rights lawsuit. (Southwestern Oblate Historical Archives.)

to the fundamental principle that racial discrimination in public education is unconstitutional." Later that year, in October, the Texas Supreme Court ruled that local school districts could proceed with desegregation efforts "without regard to state laws."

Integration in America's schools did not fully occur until the 1960s and 1970s, but if a 1930 Del Rio court decision had been upheld, the Civil Rights Era would have started in Del Rio 24 years before the U.S. Supreme *Court's Brown* v. *Board of Education* decisions.

The court case concerning civil rights of Mexican-Americans, known as [Del Rio] *Independent School District* v. *Salvatierra* (1930), dealt with school resources, racial identity, and pedagogical methods—and segregation within the public schools. In Texas, the segregation of Mexican-Americans was not a statewide policy but segregation was done rather at the local school districts. There was also general ethnic prejudice that forced ethnic Mexicans-Americans into sub-standard, and definitely unequal, schools.

The Salvatierra case was the first case to ask for judicial review of school district actions concerning the education of Mexican-Americans. The Del Rio ISD operated a campus with four buildings: three at one end of the property and one at the other end. The three, one high school and two elementary buildings, were reserved for Anglos, and the other, a two-room structure, was reserved for "Mexicans." The two sides of the campus were separated by an athletic field. A plan to expand the facilities, announced January 7, 1930, would add a new senior high building and enlarge the elementary school buildings; it would also add

Mexican School, Del Rio, Tex.

Again, identification is uncertain, but the postcard caption suggests that even though the facilities are improved, segregation continued.

five rooms to the Mexican school. (In the various newspaper reports, the school was not referred to as the "Mexican" school formally, but as the West End Elementary School.)

The issue of the case was the equal protection clause of the Constitution's Fourteenth Amendment. The parents "were not questioning the quality of the facilities," but they were claiming that the segregation of ethnic Mexicans from the rest of the student population denied their children "the right and privilege of mingling with those of the other races in the common enjoyment of identical school facilities, instruction, associations, and environment."

The trial court supported the parents. The court granted an injunction against the school district, prohibiting ethnic segregation. While often tedious, the language of the court's decision was unmistakable. The school system was prohibited from denying full school access to children of Hispanic descent. The school system was prohibited from offering a lesser quality of facilities to children of Hispanic descent. The school system was also prohibited from denying "the equal rights, privileges, opportunities, uses, benefits, facilities, conveniences and instructions" to children of Hispanic descent.

The language of the court's decision did not focus on constitutional rights; although, it eventually got to that point. Rather, the decision focused on Texas legislative acts, and "non-acts." The state legislature had not passed a law authorizing school districts to segregate "one class of white children from another." Therefore, the judge continued, "such segregation by the Defendants is in violation of the Fourteenth Amendment to the Constitution of the United States."

The appellate court, however, rejected the parents' claims and district court's decision in favor of the argument of the school district. Having lost the trial, the school district had appealed to the Fourth Court of Appeals in San Antonio. The court there ruled that the school board for DRISD "had not gone beyond the administrative powers delegated to it by constitutional and statutory provisions." The court's opinion was that school boards were not supposed to segregate students on the basis of ethnicity, but such was not the situation in this case. School districts were allowed to separate Mexican students from the general population for reasons other than ethnicity, reasons generally labeled as instructional.

The school district argument, accepted by the appellate court, was that the Mexican school was there on the grounds of "late enrollment," "irregular attendance" (due to a significant migrant population), and "the language problem." And concerning the DRISD school officials specifically, the court ruled that they had not gone beyond their administrative powers. "Thus, in this first important legal challenge to racial discrimination in the public schools," as civil rights author Guadalupe San Miguel Jr. has written, "the court stipulated that it was unconstitutional to segregate Mexican students based on national origin grounds, but it did allow segregation on educational grounds."

The status quo would remain, and the Civil Rights Era would have to wait for the case from Topeka, Kansas.

The segregation issue returned to Del Rio in 1949, when the Texas State Department of Education revoked Del Rio ISD's accreditation. The Del Rio ISD operated two campuses at that time: north campus and south campus. The railroad tracks passing through town represented the boundary line between the two. The south campus still had four buildings, of which two were reserved for ethnic Mexicans.

All Mexican students in the south district attended south campus, but Mexican students in the north campus area also attended the south campus' Mexican school. White, or non-Hispanic, students attended the nearest elementary school.

The administrative action was based on a court ruling made during the summer of 1948: *Delgado v. Bastrop ISD*, the first such case since Del Rio's 1930 case. Judge Ben H. Rice found that the school district violated the Fourteenth Amendment rights of Mexican-American students with its segregation policy. (This is essentially what the Del Rio plaintiffs had claimed 18 years earlier.) The ruling "permanently restrained and enjoined from segregation pupils of Mexican or other Latin American descent."

State Superintendent of Education L.A. Woods then issued instructions to all public schools in Texas. First, segregation of Latin Americans in separate classes or schools was forbidden. Separate classes "on the same campus" were permissible for instructional purposes, but all students were to have full access to all school facilities and programs. And all school administrative personnel were to take "all necessary steps to eliminate any and all segregation" within Texas schools and districts.

Later that year, a complaint was filed with the State Department of Education by Del Rioan Cristobal Aldrete. In response, Assistant State Superintendent T.M. Trimble inspected the district; he found that Mexican-Americans were only allowed to teach in the "Mexican" schools and that each building housed students of only one of the two groups. Superintendent Woods acted on Trimble's recommendation by revoking the DRISD's accreditation on February 12, 1949, on the grounds of continued segregation of Mexican students for reasons other than instructional. According to Woods, "segregation which has existed within the Del Rio School for the . . . past many years has existed with no particular excuse except that separation of the two ethnic groups of children."

In response, the state legislature stripped Superintendent Woods of his authority. The powers of office were transferred to a new appointed office of commissioner of education. J.W. Edgar, the new commissioner, held another hearing on the Del Rio matter and then reversed the decision, restoring accreditation to Del Rio ISD.

The commissioner of education issued new guidelines stating that "any form of segregation not authorized by the [Texas] Constitution" was impermissible. However, the guidelines stated that complaints of segregation of Hispanic students were to be forwarded to local school boards. In effect, the state commissioner announced that the state government would not interfere with local authority. Segregation remained acceptable and legal.

During the 1960s and 1970s, school integration became one of the most explosive issues in American politics, and Del Rio was not immune. The city of Del Rio was the location, once again, of a serious dispute about segregation within public schools. The resolution was the consolidation of two independent school systems: one Hispanic and one predominantly Anglo. But the most unusual part about the court case is that, generally speaking, when it went to court it was the Anglos who were more in favor of integration while the Hispanics were opposed.

Del Rio's third venture into the Civil Rights Movement actually came by way of East Texas and a federal judge named William Wayne Justice. Judge Justice had ordered the consolidation of several small school districts with predominantly black student bodies into larger, wealthier, predominantly white school districts in an effort to provide the black students with more equitable educational opportunities. Meanwhile the Department of Defense began pushing for some kind of resolution to a local situation involving students living at Laughlin Air Force Base. Laughlin was situated within the boundaries of San Felipe ISD, but the parents sent their children to schools in the Del Rio ISD. This put the Air Force in the position of appearing to support segregation. Air Force representatives suggested consolidation, but this was rejected by officials in both ISDs. During the 1970–1971 school year, Del Rio ISD taught about 4,500 students (48 percent Hispanics, 48 percent Anglos, and 4 percent blacks) including Laughlin's 729 (87 percent Anglo, 6.5 percent Hispanic, and 6.5 percent black). San Felipe ISD taught about 2,200 (98 percent Hispanic and 2 percent black).

On July 16, 1971, the DRISD school board president, Hi Newby, received word from Judge Justice that transferring students from SFISD (particularly Laughlin) to DRISD would end. The effects of this order caused great disturbances in both districts. DRISD had built new schools with the expectation of accommodating more than 700 military dependent students. SFISD's classrooms were already overcrowded and would not be able to house a dramatic increase in student population. Rumors circulated throughout Del Rio that the Air Force would close Laughlin if the situation was not resolved.

The public on both sides of San Felipe Creek dug in their heels in opposition to the various outside pressures. By July 30, though, the DRISD school board approved a resolution to ask Judge Justice to consolidate the two districts. Consolidation could only happen if voted on and approved by majorities in both school districts or ordered by a judge. Nearly everyone conceded that a vote would fail in both districts.

August 6, 1971, was the big day when Judge Justice ordered consolidation less than a month after the issue was put on the table as a serious alternative. However, the order required consolidation to be completed before the 1971–72 school year began, just four weeks off. When school began on September 7, the San Felipe Del Rio Consolidated Independent School District (a name change ordered by Judge Justice) came into being. All of the regular high school activities were disrupted to some extent or another. The two school mascots—the San Felipe Mustangs and Del Rio Wildcats—were replaced with a new mascot, one supported by many of the students: the Rams. The new colors of blue and white were chosen, and

The original high school building was replaced in the 1930s with this building now known as Old Del Rio High. The building has been used as a middle school since the new high school was built on the north side of town in the late 1960s (just before consolidation).

the old school colors—maroon and gold, and purple and gold—became part of history. New uniforms, songs, and yearbook names all had to be adopted.

Problems large and small afflicted the consolidated district. Students missed busses and parents missed students as a result of a new pick-up and drop-off schedule. Students were taken out of their comfort zones as they attended schools outside of their immediate neighborhoods. Some protests and vandalism occurred, but on the whole there was no violence. The following school year (1972–1973) found the townspeople adjusting and becoming accustomed to the new realities.

The consolidation created a new school district, but it eliminated two others. The alumni of one of the old districts, San Felipe, have recognized that without a concerted effort, history will disappear. In 1979, graduates of San Felipe High organized the "San Felipe Exes of Del Rio," but no corresponding organization has formed for the old Del Rio school district. The Exes later purchased land for the San Felipe Exes Memorial Center, which was dedicated in 1985. The property is the old residence of Santos Garza, who led the founding of the San Felipe ISD. The house was built by stonemason John Taini, who built so many of Del Rio's oldest structures. The center is a museum and meeting place reminding visitors of life and education in the San Felipe schools.

As Del Rio grew northward across the railroad track, Hill Elementary School was built to serve families there. The northern part of Del Rio sits at a higher elevation than the older part of town along San Felipe Creek; consequently, the north part of town is sometimes called "the Hill."

13. Main Street

Like many Texas towns, Del Rio's growth has drawn the population outward—away from the city's center. Much of the new development is along "the highway," in Del Rio's case, U.S. Highway 90 (and 277). In town this highway includes Avenue F, which will be renamed Veterans Boulevard by the time this book is in print.

Del Rioans have on occasion made efforts to remember the city's history: the San Felipe Exes, Fiesta de Amistad, the Whitehead Memorial Museum, and the Val Verde County Historical Commission's historical markers. In 2002, a new program combining historical preservation and economic redevelopment has been added to these efforts.

The Main Street Program has been called "the best value per public dollar invested in Texas," by former Lieutenant Governor Bob Bullock. However, it is not some giant, massive government program that generates statewide or national news. Instead, some 125 Texas towns (to date) have invested time, money, and a great deal of elbow grease to improve their hometowns by cleaning, repairing, and restoring their downtown business communities and bringing new life to Hometown Texas.

The idea behind Main Street is to find the town's character, those elements that make it unique and special, and capitalize on that character. The program participants restore and rehabilitate vacant buildings, encourage entrepreneurs to move back into the downtown, and market the downtown as a unique shopping and living experience. Historical preservation is the "means," and economic revitalization is the "ends." To date, the statistics show that Main Street has created nearly 5,000 businesses with over 18,000 employees and, in the process, some 8,000 historic buildings have been restored to use.

Del Rio became a Main Street city on January 1, 2002, so the work has just begun. The First Lady of Texas Anita Perry visited Del Rio on February 25th to kick off the project and raise public awareness. The remaining portion of this chapter consists of photographs of Del Rio's Main Street in days past. Most date to times before the Second World War, and some may date to the years immediately following the First World War. Many readers will remember these scenes; many probably shopped in these stores.

By way of advertising the Val Verde County Historical Commission, the commission is gathering things historical about the Main Street area: photographs, papers, and memories. You might know some history that no one else has mentioned, and so your memories and your words can become part of Del Rio's recorded history. The Val Verde County Historical Commission and the Main Street Program both will welcome greater community participation.

Now, here are the photos of Del Rio's historic downtown Main Street:

The Main Street area is composed of two major parts. This aerial photograph focuses on the industrial downtown from the railroad reserve, at top and top right, to Garfield, the street crossing from center left to bottom right. The industrial downtown included the railroad facilities including the roundhouse, passenger depot, freight depot, and the various sheds. It also includes buildings that once were hotels, such as the Henson Hotel, now Wipff's Furniture, as well as warehouse and freight companies. (Warren Studio.)

This lower angle shot shows the area between Main, at right, and Griner, at top left. The area where City Hall now resides was residential. The hotel across from Wipff's is now a shed and cell phone tower. This photo dates to the 1920s. (Warren Studio.)

The southwest corner of Main and Losoya is occupied by the Foster Building. A bank occupied the ground level—the safe is supposed to still be in the building. The second floor was occupied by offices. The building immediately to the south housed a pharmacy, jeweler, and bargain store. (Warren Studio.)

The Del Rio News-Herald *occupied this building on the northwest corner of Main and Broadway (across from the Old Federal Building) until its move to Bedell. The building was encased in blue sheet metal. Other Main Street programs have discovered that such sheathing sometimes actually preserves the brick and/or stonework underneath. It may be that this same classic downtown business brick architecture may be waiting to be brought out. The Electric Bakery on the corner and Beadle's Ice Cream Parlor probably catered to federal employees across the street. (Warren Studio.)*

The block south of Canal begins the transition from the Main Street business district (with smaller structures) to the residential area of South Del Rio. I am still wondering what a "Hupmobile"—on the sign at Dobkins Garage—is. (Warren Studio.)

The Princess sat were Casa de Mimi #1 now resides. Note the Mae West movie being advertised, one of her more famous films. The Princess was one of Del Rio's more plush establishments and is reported to be the place were the Texas Sheep and Goat Raisers Association was organized in 1915. (Warren Studio.)

This is a balcony-level view of the block between Garfield and Losoya. Note the windmill repair shop at left and Lippe's Studio further back. Robert Warren (of Warren Studio) bought out Lippe in 1941. Lippe may have bought out Noah Rose (who had a studio on the same block, but who left Del Rio in 1919), whose name appears on some of Del Rio's oldest photos. Beauty shops, bakeries, real estate offices, hotels, record shops, and banks all appear on this one block. (Warren Studio.)

This photo (though in better shape than the previous) was shot at an earlier time. The six-story First National Building has not yet been built. The Warner Building, dominant at left, had offices upstairs, including that of dentist L.H. Rogers. (Warren Studio.)

The Main Street District includes part of Pecan Street. This is the Old Elks Hall on the northeast corner of Pecan and Losoya, across from the county courthouse. Now called the Pecan Street Station, the 1916 structure includes a grand ballroom upstairs and was a popular social setting for formal dances and gambling. (Warren Studio.)

This aerial view shows a pair of automobiles at bottom center, each turning left around each other instead of in front of one another. Garfield is the dividing line between the industrial downtown and the commercial downtown. The commercial downtown includes businesses catering to Del Rioans and the local community rather than travelers and railroaders. The old City Hall is on Garfield at top right, and the long buildings north and east of it are the Eagle Pass Lumber Company sheds. (Warren Studio.)

The Ross Building, on the southwest corner of Main and Canal, is an example of what can be done with a historic building. The structure was a drugstore when it was built at the turn of the century. Doctors' offices occupied the second story, which was added later. In 1991, H.B. Ross's grandson Jim Sanders and wife Betty bought the building, removed non-sympathetic alterations, and opened the Emporium Ice Cream and Soda Bar. (Warren Studio.)

Another Pecan Street building is the International Order of Odd Fellows Building on Pecan and Cactus. It was once used as office space for Rose Dawn and Koran, astrologers advertising on John Brinkley's Radio XERA during the 1930s. The building is now occupied by AOL-TimeWarner Cable. (Warren Studio.)

The St. Charles Hotel was the next building on the block. It burned some 50 years ago, which is ironic, since the owners had advertised the Roswell, their newer hotel, as air conditioned and fireproof. This photo shows the Main Street block between Losoya and Greenwood—looking northward. (Warren Studio.)

This photo shows much of the same block, looking southward. Drugstores, cafes, a barber shop, billiard hall, and insurance office occupied the various buildings, some of which are now vacant. Note the location of the Princess Theater. (Warren Studio.)

The First National Bank replaced its two-story structure with this five-story structure in 1928—but went bankrupt in 1931, a victim of the Great Depression. Del Rio National Bank bought the assets and reopened the bank under its own name. During the 1960s and 1970s, Del Rio National bought the remaining buildings on the block. (Warren Studio.)

This is the two-story stone building originally housing the First National Bank, one of Del Rio's four early banks. (Warren Studio.)

This image shows the block south of Greenwood with Woolworth's on the southeast corner and Del Rio National Bank in its home from 1910 to 1931 on the southwest. The Del Rio National Bank building was designed by Alfred Giles, a noted San Antonio architect. The Guarantee was then smaller and known as Stool's Store, on the left, and several wooden buildings were still in use, on the right. (Warren Studio.)

This structure sits on the southwest corner of Main and Broadway. The transom windows indicate that the buildings pre-date air conditioning. The near business is a Piggly-Wiggly. The chamber of commerce used to occupy the center of the block. The site at the end of the building is currently occupied by Warren Studio, now owned by Rosie Calvetti, who provided the bulk of the photographs in this book. (Warren Studio.)

The Warner Building on the northeast corner of Main and Losoya, now occupied by Sam's Boot Corral, was once J.C. Penney's. The earliest known business here was a Norvell-March Department Store. It was also E.S. Block's Groceries and Hardware, Brothers, and a Mill Outlet. The office space upstairs once housed part of Dr. Brinkley's medical practice. The building was constructed in 1905 by Italian stonemason John Taini. (Warren Studio.)

The Old Montgomery Ward Building on the 700 block is one of the more prominent buildings on the south end of the Main Street business district, between Greenwood and Canal. The building has recently been put to use with a new business and is featured in Texas Historical Commission sketches as an example of how Del Rio buildings might be restored to their classic lines. (Warren Studio.)

Roach-McLymont's on the southwest corner of Main and Canal was once Del Rio's most comprehensive department store. The business was started in 1896 and moved to this location in 1901. Dry goods, groceries, cosmetics, fancy women's wear, and toys all had their place. Roach's, as it was commonly called, also included a gasoline station, meat market, and soda fountain. (Warren Studio.)

The district continues down Main Street to Academy and along Academy across the creek to Brown Plaza. The neighborhood plaza is named for George Washington Brown, who crossed the Isthmus of Panama during Gold Rush days and returned east to live with his family in Texas. This photograph from the 1970s shows the grass that was later replaced with brick. (Charles Carlson)

The plaza is the site for celebrations such as Diez y Seis and Cinco de Mayo and was also the principal business district in the San Felipe neighborhood. All of these buildings were severely damaged by the Flood of 1998. The building at the north end had been used as a cultural arts center, La Casa de la Cultura, and was rebuilt by the City of Del Rio in 2002. (Texas Historical Commission.)

Many buildings in the Main Street District have had several lives. Piggly Wiggly was once housed near the Old Federal Building, but it also resided here—wherever here is. History is often a detective story. Finding clues in a photo or linking one image with another are part of the chase. The storefront materials shown here are very reflective and images from across the street are reflected. "Hotel S" appears to be the sign reflected in the top left corner of the storefront. The reflection also shows a roofline.

Refer to the top photograph on page 147. The left skyline shows a roofline on the St. Charles Hotel Building. It matches the reflection. Look to the right (east) line of buildings, just to the left from the "Walgreen Agency, Dick's Drugs" sign. A storefront there has a series of white, upright triangles—which match the white, upright triangles above the name "Piggly Wiggly" in this photograph. This photo places the grocery store across Losoya Street from the Warner Building (Sam's Boot Corral).

BIBLIOGRAPHY

BOOKS

Albro, Ward S. *Always a Rebel: Ricardo Flores Magón and the Mexican Revolution*. Fort Worth: Texas Christian University Press, 1992.

Allsup, Carl. *The American G.I. Forum: Origins and Evolution*. Austin: University of Texas Press, 1982.

Austerman, Wayne R. *Sharps Rifles and Spanish Mules: The San Antonio–El Paso Mail, 1851–1881*. College Station: Texas A&M University Press, 1985.

Bolton, Herbert Eugene, ed. *Spanish Exploration in the Southwest: 1542–1706*. New York: Charles Scribner's Sons, 1916.

Braudaway, Douglas Lee. *Images of America: Railroads of Western Texas: San Antonio to El Paso*. Charleston, SC: Arcadia Publishing, 2000.

———. *Images of America: Val Verde County*. Charleston, SC: Arcadia Publishing, 1999.

Bryan, C.D.B. *The National Air and Space Museum*. New York: Harry N. Abrams, Inc., 1979.

Carman, Michael Dennis. *United States Customs and the Madero Revolution*. El Paso: Texas Western Press, 1976.

Carson, Gerald. *The Roguish World of Doctor Brinkley*. New York: Rinehart & Company, Inc., 1960.

Coker, Caleb, ed. *The News from Brownsville: Helen Chapman's Letters from the Texas Military Frontier, 1848–1852*. Austin: Texas State Historical Association, 1992.

De León, Arnoldo. *Mexican Americans in Texas: A Brief History*. Arlington Heights, IL: Harlan Davidson, Inc., 1993.

Fowler, Gene, and Bill Crawford. *Border Radio*. Austin: Texas Monthly Press, 1987.

Frazier, Donald S. *Blood & Treasure: Confederate Empire in the Southwest*. College Station: Texas A&M University Press, 1995.

Gournay, Luke. *Texas Boundaries: Evolution of the State's Counties*. College Station: Texas A&M University Press, 1995.

Greer, James Kimmins. *Colonel Jack Hays: Texas Frontier Leader and California Builder*. (Revised Edition). College Station: Texas A&M University Press, 1987.

Gutierrez, A.E. *A History of San Felipe*. Del Rio: Whitehead Memorial

Museum, 1978.

Hart, Herbert M. *Old Forts of the Southwest*. Seattle: Superior Publishing Company, 1964.

Henderson, Peter V.N. *Mexican Exiles in the Borderlands: 1910–1913*. El Paso: Texas Western Press, 1979.

Hofsommer, Don L. *The Southern Pacific, 1901–1985*. College Station: Texas A&M University Press, 1986.

Kerig, Dorothy Pierson. *Luther T. Ellsworth: U.S. Consul on the Border during the Mexican Revolution*. El Paso: Texas Western Press, 1975.

Kinney County Historical Society. *Kinney County: 1852–1977*. 1977.

Langham, Thomas C. *Border Trials: Ricardo Flores Magón and the Mexican Liberals*. El Paso: Texas Western Press, 1981.

Linden, Glenn M. *Desegregating Schools in Dallas: Four Decades in the Federal Courts*. Dallas: Three Forks Press, 1995.

Malsch, Brownson. *Indianola: The Mother of Western Texas*. Austin: State House Press, 1988.

The Mayans. *The Revelation Secret*. San Antonio: Naylor Press, 1935–1936.

Mehling, Harold. *The Scandalous Scamps*. New York: Henry Holt and Company, 1959.

Mel-Roy, Dr. *Book of Dreams*. Privately published.

Miller, Tom. *On the Border: Portraits of America's Southwestern Frontier*. New York: Harper & Row, Publishers, 1981.

Montgomery, Cora. (Pseudonym for Mrs. William L Cazneau.) *Eagle Pass, or Life on the Border*. Austin: Pemberton Press, 1966. (Reprint of 1852 edition.)

Morris, Sam. *Drink and the Downfall of Nations*. Grand Rapids, MI: Zondervan Publishing House, 1945.

Muney, Analeslie. *Texas Municipal Election Law Manual, Third Edition*. Texas Municipal Clerks Association, Inc., 1997.

Newcomb, W.W., Jr. *The Indians of Texas: From Prehistoric to Modern Times*. Austin: University of Texas Press, 1961. Fourth Printing, 1967.

Olmstead, Frederick Law. *A Journey through Texas: Or, a Saddle-Trip on the Spanish Frontier*. Austin: University of Texas Press, 1978 (1857).

Overfelt, Robert. *The Val Verde Winery: Its Role in Texas Viticulture and Enology*. El Paso: Texas Western Press, 1985.

Pocock, Chris. *Dragon Lady: The History of the U-2 Spyplane*. England: Airlife, 1989.

Polmar, Norman. *Spyplane: The U-2 History Declassified*. China: MBI Publishing Company, 2001.

Reed, S.G. *A History of the Texas Railroads*. New York: Arno Press, 1981.

San Miguel, Guadalupe, Jr. *"Let All of Them Take Heed": Mexican Americans and the Campaign for Educational Equality in Texas, 1910–1981*. Austin: University of Texas, 1987.

Santleben, August. *A Texas Pioneer: Early Staging and Overland Freighting Days on the Frontiers of Texas and Mexico*. New York: Neale Publishing Company, 1994.

Savage, Candace. *Eagles of North America*. Ashland, WI: NorthWord Inc., 1987.

Shafer, Harry J. *Ancient Texans: Rock Art and Lifeways along the Lower Pecos.* Texas Monthly Press, 1986.

Skiles, Jack. *Judge Roy Bean Country.* Lubbock: Texas Tech University, 1996.

Sonnichsen, C.L. *Roy Bean: Law West of the Pecos.* New York: Macmillan, 1943.

Strickland, Ron. *Texans: Oral Histories from the Lone Star State.* New York: Paragon House, 1991.

Swift, Roy L. *Three Roads to Chihuahua: The Great Wagon Roads That Opened the Southwest, 1823–1883.* Austin: Eakin Press, 1988.

Terrell County Historical Commission. *Terrell County, Texas: Its Past, Its People.* San Angelo: Anchor Publishing Company, 1978.

Whitehead Memorial Museum and Val Verde County Historical Commission. *La Hacienda.* 1976.

Williams, Clayton W. *Texas' Last Frontier: Fort Stockton and the Trans-Pecos, 1861–1895.* College Station: Texas A&M University Press, 1982.

Wilson, Neill C., and Frank J. Taylor. *Southern Pacific: The Roaring Story of a Fighting Railroad.* New York: McGraw-Hill Book Company, Inc., 1952.

Zertuche, Diana Sotelo. *Spirit of Val Verde.* 1985.

ARTICLES, INTERVIEWS, PRESENTATIONS, AND MISC.

Baker, Alvin Lee. Collected clippings.

Baker, Jim. "Notes."

Baker, Michael. "Val Verde Centennial: How Did County Get Its Name?" *Del Rio Guide.* January 1985.

Beale Air Force Base. website http://www.beale.af.mil/AIRCRAFT/timeline.html.

Bender, A.B. "Opening Routes across West Texas, 1848–1850." *Southwestern Historical Quarterly.* (October 1933), Vol. 37.

Bliss, Zenas R. "The Zenas R. Bliss Papers." Volumes 1 & 2.

Boies, Ray. "Del Rio, Val Verde County, Texas: General Summary-Historical and Factual." 1925.

Braudaway, Douglas Lee. "Desegregation in Del Rio." *Journal of South Texas.* Fall 2000.

Cheaney, Frank. "Fort Clark Tour Guide Notes."

Comstock Study Club. *Comstock Friends and Neighbors.*

Crawford, Bill, Gene Fowler, and Paul Kallinger. "Border Radio." Presentation given January 24, 1998.

Dallas Morning News. Texas Almanac, 1990–1991.

Daughtrey, Elizabeth S. "Legends and Historical Facts about Round Mountain." December 1991.

Daughtrey, Robuck. "U.S. Air Force Activities in and near Del Rio, Val Verde County, Texas." 1981. (Texas Historical Marker Commission).

Daughtrey, Elizabeth and Robuck. Interview. October 25, 1996.

Del Rio, City of. City Charters.

———. City Council Minutes.

"Del Rio: 'The City of Roses.' " *Sheep and Goat Raisers' Magazine.* February 1922.

Elliott, Claude. "The Building of the Southern Pacific Railroad through Texas." Master's thesis. University of Texas at Austin. June 1928.

English, Sarah Jane. "Val Verde Winery Celebrates a Century." *Texas Highways*. January 1984.

Faulkner, Walter A. "With Sibley in New Mexico: The Journal of William Henry Smith." *West Texas Historical Association Yearbook*. (Vol. 27). October 1951.

Fowler, Gene. "Queen City of the Rio Grande." *Texas Highways*. March 1995.

Garabedian, Charles A. "The Wildcats vs. the Mustangs: The Consolidation of the San Felipe and Del Rio Independent School Districts." Master's thesis. Sul Ross State University. 1994.

Guys, Carl. Interview. March 25, 1997.

Handbook of Texas. (1996 Edition.)

International Boundary Commission, American Section. *Special Flood Report: Flood of September and October 1932*. International Portion of the Rio Grande, El Paso, 1932.

International Boundary and Water Commission. *Amistad Dam and Reservoir Project*.

James, Vinton Lee. *Frontier and Pioneer Recollections of Early Days in San Antonio and West Texas*. San Antonio: Artes Graficas, 1938. (Published by the author.)

Kerrigan, William T. "Race, Expansion, and Slavery in Eagle Pass, Texas, 1852." *Southwestern Historical Quarterly*. January 1998.

Kochan, J.P., P.S. Kochan, and T. Kusiak. "Estudio de la Comunidad Ciudad Acuña, Coahuila, Mexico."

Krapf, Kellie A., and Sharlene N. Allday. "The Historic Period in the Lower Pecos River and Val Verde County Region." *Prehistoric and Historic Overview of the Laughlin Air Force Base Area: Del Rio, Val Verde County, and the Lower Pecos Region (10,000 B.C. to A.D. 1942)*.

Lammons, Frank Bishop. "Operation Camel: An Experiment in Animal Transportation in Texas, 1857–1860." *Southwestern Historical Quarterly*. July 1957.

Mallory, Randy. "Ribbons of Steel." *Texas Highways*. May 1994.

Martin, Mabelle Eppard. "California Emigrant Roads through Texas." *Southwestern Historical Quarterly*. April 1925.

Montague, Brian. "The San Felipe Agricultural, Manufacturing & Irrigation Company of Del Rio, Texas." 1972. Manuscript on file at Val Verde Historical Commission.

National Air and Space Museum. ceps.nasm.edu/PA/NASMNEWS/VinFiz.html.

Nelson, Al B. "Juan De Ugalde and Picax-Ande Ins-Tinsle: 1787–1788." *Southwestern Historical Quarterly*. April 1940.

Office of History. Laughlin A.F.B. "A Brief History of Laughlin AFB and the 47th Flying Training Wing." 1995.

Peña, Jaime. "A History of the San Felipe Independent School District and Its Influence on the Community, 1929–1951." Master's thesis. Sul Ross State University. August 1951.

Perkins, George O. "The Early History of Val Verde County." Master's thesis. Sul Ross State University. January 1954.

Pingenot, Ben. "Fort Clark, Texas: A Brief History." *The Journal of Big Bend Studies.* Volume VII, January 1995.

Poole, O.B., Jr. Interview. May 23, 1998.

Rangel, Jorge C., and Carlos M. Alcala. "Project Report: De Jure Segregation of Chicanos in Texas Schools." *Harvard Civil Rights-Civil Liberties Law Review.* Volume 7, Number 2, March 1972.

Schmidt, Leslie. Interview. April 15, 1998.

Seale, Axcie C. "The Writings and Collected Papers of Mrs. Axcie C. Seale, Texas State Historical Survey Committee Member."

Seale, Axcie. "A History of Val Verde County." April 1945.

Sellers, Rosella R. "The History of Fort Duncan, Eagle Pass, Texas." Master's thesis. Sul Ross State University.

Signor, John R. "SP's West Texas Mountain Division: A Survey of Operations El Paso to Del Rio." *Trainline.* No. 47, (Spring 1996).

Simpton, Jerry. Presentation to Del Rio City Council. August 8, 2000.

Torres, Frank E. Interview. October 19, 1996.

United States Bureau of the Census, 13th Census, 1910, Volume 131, Val Verde County, Texas.

United States Congress. Hearings before the Subcommittee on Inter-American Affairs of the Committee on Foreign Affairs, House of Representatives, 86th Congress, Second Session on H.R. 8080. U.S. Government Printing Office: Washington, D.C., 1960.

United States National Park Service. *Amistad National Recreation Area: Cultural Resources Study.* October 1994.

Val Verde County. Commissioners Court Minutes.

————. Deed Records.

————. Election Records.

Val Verde County Historical Commission. "Data About San Felipe Springs, Creek and the San Felipe Irrigation System, Del Rio, Val Verde County, Texas."

Vineyard, Bonney. Interview. September 17, 1996.

Werner, George C. "Sunset Route Centennial." *National Railway Bulletin.* (Vol. 48). 1983.

Woods, John Price. Interview. March 22, 1998.

NEWSPAPERS

Del Rio *Evening News.*

Del Rio *News Herald.*

Laughlin A.F.B. *Border Eagle.*

Louisville (Kentucky) *Courier-Journal.*

New York Times.

San Antonio *Express-News.*

San Antonio *Light.*

San Antonio *Weekly Express News.*

INDEX

159

Val Verde County's first economic activity was agriculture. Del Rio and its surroundings were home to many farms, ranches, orchards, and dairies, including Gulick's. Note the three-digit telephone number on the side of the horse-drawn cart. (Warren Studio.)